first digs

the

quasi-adult's

guide to

decorating

with style—

without

blowing

your

budget

first digs

yee-fan sun

produced by the philip lief group, inc.

St. Martin's Griffin
New York

The anecdotes contained in this book have been created as a didactic tool. While some accurately describe actual case histories, most have been formed by combining aspects of several different cases and life experiences in the author's and writer's lives in order to highlight particular points in the text.

www.stmartins.com

Produced by The Philip Lief Group, Inc.
Managing Editors: Judy Linden and Albry Montalbano

Book *design by rlf design*

All illustrations © 2005 Yee-Fan Sun, except as follows: pages 32, 96 © 2004 Drew Erickson and Nicole Washington; pages 92, 133 © 2004 Erin Fournier; pages 32, 120 © 2004 Darleen Lev; pages 32, 122 © 2004 Megan Scott Verzi.

Text contributors: Diana Goodman (Chapter 8, wall painting); Gretchen Schaefer (Chapter 8, spray painting); Donna Wilson (Chapter 12, weeding plan, culling school stuff).

Library of Congress Cataloging-in-Publication Data

Sun, Yee-Fan.
    First digs : the quasi-adult's guide to decorating with style—without blowing your budget / Yee-Fan Sun.
        p. cm.
    ISBN 0-312-34728-6
    EAN 978-0-312-34728-4
    1. Handicraft 2. House furnishings. 3. Interior decoration. I. Title.

TT157.S8485 2006
747—dc22   2006040973

First Edition: May 2006

10 9 8 7 6 5 4 3 2 1

To all the DigsMagazine.com readers and especially

my fellow Digsters on the boards: Thanks for

making work seem like play, and for turning a little

corner of the Web world into a place

that feels like home.

contents

acknowledgments

This book would not have been possible without Judy Linden and Albry Montalbano at The Philip Lief Group, and Sheila Curry Oakes at St. Martin's Press. It has been a joy and a privilege to work with them, and I am deeply grateful for all their support, advice, insight, and hard work.

Many thanks as well to the following writers, whose articles first appeared on DigsMagazine.com and now contribute to portions of this book: Diana Goodman ("Painting 101," originally published July 30, 2001, and August 13, 2001), Gretchen Schaefer ("Say It with Spray Paint," originally published August 27, 2001), and Donna Wilson ("On Weeding," originally published May 29, 2000). I would also like to acknowledge the folks who generously shared photos of their homes, first in the Open House feature on DigsMagazine.com and now in this book: Drew Erickson and Nicole Washington, Erin Fournier, Darleen Lev, and Megan Scott Verzi.

Finally, a special word of thanks to my parents and brothers, with whom I so happily shared digs for the first eighteen or so years of my life, and to my husband, Asher, in whose company I always feel at home, even as we bounce from one far corner of the world to the next.

honey, i'm home!

for most of us, it happens not long after graduation day: With memories of flying tassels, commencement speeches, and teary farewells still fresh in our minds, we find ourselves saying another good-bye. Back in the familiar bedrooms where we brooded through high school and lazed through college vacations, we notice the fading band posters and magazine cutout collages—and realize that we've outgrown more than that tiny twin bed; we've outgrown our childhood home. It's a monumental event when we realize we're ready to move out of the parental nest for good. Thrust suddenly into the big scary adult world, however, it takes a while before we begin to settle in and make a real home. Whether you're a guy or a girl, slaving away at your first job or going to grad school, living in the city, the 'burbs, or the country, creating a home that doesn't resemble your old college dorm turns out to be hard work. *First Digs* is here to help.

When I graduated from college, I left with a magna cum laude in visual and environmental studies and not a semblance of where to go next. In a dedicated effort to avoid making a decision about my future, I spent the next couple of years bouncing from one far-flung place to another—from D.C., to Italy, Australia, and beyond. But when the nomadic life began to lose its appeal, I made the first big decision of my postcollege life. I retrieved the stuff I'd been storing in my parents' Massachusetts basement and moved to Tucson, Arizona—in the name of love, and with the hopes that leaving the familiar comforts of home might be exactly the kick in the pants I needed. The move proved successful on both counts. As my boyfriend, now husband, and I eagerly dove into the task of setting up our first semipermanent home, I discovered a dearth of good home and living resources geared at recent grads like us—and promptly set out to create one myself. DigsMagazine.com was launched in January 2000, delivering down-to-earth home talk with a healthy side of humor. I figured my friends at least would get a kick out of my tales of DIY successes and fix-up projects gone horribly awry; what I discovered was that there were a whole lot of other quasi-adult men and women who shared my fears, dilemmas, and obsessions with setting up house. Over the years, the site has spawned a lively and devoted message boards community whose many regulars have even given themselves a name. Calling themselves Digsters, they tell me that at *Digs*, they've found a place that feels like home.

Like the Web site, *First Digs* aims to make the transition from college housing to first apartment a little easier and a lot more fun. Offering practical how-tos and step-by-step tutorials that even the most domestically impaired can successfully tackle, this book teaches you those important adult-world homemaking skills that you wish you'd learned in school: overcoming decorating inertia, scoring great furnishings at a sweet price, figuring out what to do with your goods after you've heaved them home, embracing the DIY spirit even if you've never picked up a sewing needle or a drill in your life, and keeping it all looking presentable once you've crafted a nest that's chock full of your own gloriously unique personality. Ultimately, *First Digs* offers both the utilitarian skills of apartment spruce-up and the inspiration to create a home in which you can live these post-college years to the fullest.

first digs

choose your own (living) adventure

t was so easy back in the college dorm days. Fill out some forms, submit them to the random gods of housing assignment, cross your fingers, and hope for the best. In the post-dorm phase of life, however, finding a roof over your head involves just a little more work. Sure, your parents dropped hints aplenty about how you're always welcome to move back into your old bedroom—and hey, maybe you've even taken them up on the offer, bunking down in your twin bed and biding time while you wait for some sign regarding what to do next. But when you get tired of sneaking your significant other out of your bedroom each morning, when Mom tells you one too many times to drive carefully as you leave to meet your friends in the city, when the Pearl Jam poster that you tacked above your bed back in eighth grade comes tumbling down atop your head one night, you'll know: It's time to strike out on your own and get your first real apartment.

But before you start packing up that moving van, there are just a few things you'll need to consider. Should you throw in your lot with some roommates, brave it solo, or maybe move in with your sweetie? How much rent is too much? And how do you know when you've found the right apartment, anyway? With questions aplenty dancing in your head, a tiny knot of panic begins to build. But quit hyperventilating: We're here to help you find your way.

share and share alike: living with roomies

When you've lived your whole life thus far in the hivelike coziness of a dorm or the family nest, the outside world can seem like a big, lonely place. Jumping straight into your own digs seems particularly intimidating when a quick glance through the newspaper rental ads reveals that for an alarmingly large chunk of your rather modest monthly salary, you can live in a closet, in a basement, or in a part of town you'd be scared to drive through in broad daylight. The solution to your predicament? Get thee some roommates.

Sharing digs with other folks means you can get a much bigger, much nicer place than you would likely be able to afford all by your lonesome. Other costs of living become cheaper as well; running utilities for two costs about the same for one, and with other people around to potentially split kitchen duties, you might find you're a whole lot more likely to actually cook in-house rather than resort to overpriced takeout.

Even if the quirks of your college housing lottery have made you leery of having to deal with roommates ever again, living with roommates in the postschool years really *can* be a good thing for more than just your economic state. Yeah, so that nice girl you bunked with freshmen year turned out to be a raging klepto and pathological liar, and the former friend you lived with the following year drove you bonkers with her tendency to pilfer your Ring Dings, but these days, you're older, wiser, and most of all, more experienced: You know a little something about what you are really looking for in a roommate.

Now if you haven't already experienced the problems of living with good friends, you might think your safest bet is to move in with someone you know and love. But think long and hard before you leap into a lease with your oldest, best friend. Fuming when your buddy takes fifty minutes in the bathroom each morning, getting passive-aggressive about the ever-present stack of someone else's dirty dishes, getting nagged when you forget (okay, again) that it's your turn to take out the trash: This is the stuff that's ruined many a fine friendship. There's way too much that can go awry when folks who have a great time hanging out together decide to share a roof . . . without taking that all-important step of considering each person's actual living style first.

Some of my very favorite people in the world are a little wacky. They keep strange hours, voluntarily getting up to tap away on their laptops in the wee hours of the night, doing a three-hour nap/three-hour wake schedule, or going days on end without any bedtime at all. They have bizarre hobbies that make their homes look like little museums of their personal obsessions. They're always finding themselves in some crazy situation with some new guy, or new girl, or every once in a blue moon, both. They're full of marvelous little quirks that make them endless sources of fascinating stories, and I always look forward to spending time with them. And a big part of the reason this is possible is because I don't have to live with their nuttiness day in and day out. And they don't have to put up with mine.

Seriously, the qualities that you look for in a friend (fun, funny, always up to something interesting) aren't necessarily the same ones you should seek in a roommate (of the same cleanliness level as you, able to pay all bills on time and willing to do so of their own volition). Yes, sometimes good friends can make great roommates, particularly if both you and the friend-cum-potential-roomie are the sort of adaptable, low-maintenance individuals who are blessed with the amazing ability not to let other people's weirdnesses bug you. But unless you're fully confident that you and your pals genuinely share similar views on such mundane matters as washing dishes, vacuuming, noise levels, and fiscal responsibility, it's often safer to keep your friends as friends and look elsewhere for someone to share your abode.

When you're moving in with a stranger, it's a beautiful clean slate: No one is bringing any baggage into the situation, allowing you all to be much more open from the very beginning about what you expect. You don't have to feel like a total jerk when you tell your stranger-roomie that you're not real keen on significant others becoming nonpaying tenants, the way you might feel if this were your good friend instead and you were talking about her boyfriend who you already knew and liked. Money issues are also way less uncomfortable to broach with people with whom you share no history. And additionally, there's the fun factor of simply getting to know a new person—who might eventually turn into as great a friend as she is a roommate, if you're lucky.

where to find 'em . . .

Once you've decided to get yourself into the roommate market, it's time to start putting out the feelers. Good, old-fashioned word-of-mouth is still the best place to start, as it's 100 percent free and involves almost no extra effort on your part. After all, you talk to people on a regular basis, don't you? Casually mention to any and everyone who'll listen that you're looking for a roommate. Your officemate might have a sister who's looking to share a pad; your mom might have a friend whose son is freaking because his roommate just bailed mid-lease. The waitress accidentally eavesdropping on your lunchtime conversation might overhear your plight and tell you that she and her roommates just happen to have an extra room in their group house that they've been trying to rent out for ages. You never know who might know someone that might just be your perfect future roommate.

While you're doing your networking, you'll also want to take more active steps to find someone to room with. When you're looking to move into your first apartment, this will likely mean finding someone who already has a specific place and is looking for someone to split the costs. The classifieds section in your local paper is the obvious place to look; you'll also want to try out online resources like craigslist.org or roommates.com, your favorite message board, and roommate matching Web sites. Neighborhood bulletin boards—in the cafe, bookstore, used CD shop, wherever—are another good potential lead. And hey, if you spy an ad at your favorite coffee hangout, you at least know that you and your potential roomie share similar tastes in java joints. Last but not least, if all else fails, you can always look to a roommate referral service for a little help from the pros.

the interview

So you've spotted a promising ad and are all geared up to take the next step. Before you reach for that telephone or shoot off an e-mail inquiry, think a little about what questions you'll need to ask. This first point of contact will be a sort of prescreening interview in which you'll want to cover the basics regarding the potential living situation, to make sure this is something that actually fits both your needs. How much is the rent? How big is the apartment or house and how many people will be living there? How old are they? (If that's important to you.) What do they do? (Likewise.) Where is the apartment located? If you have any deal-breaking issues, like smoking or pets, bring those up at the beginning as well to avoid wasting too much of your time and theirs.

If the initial phone conversation or e-mail exchange goes well, it's time to meet up in person. Anxious as you are to get your living situation settled, you might think it easiest to just get together with your prospective roomie at the apartment. And in an ideal world, where there were no potential stalkers or otherwise scary folk to contend with, you might be right. But while the vast majority of people you will encounter on your roommate search will be perfectly nice, more or less law-abiding citizens, it's better to be cautious. Set up that meeting in a public place, and let a friend know where you'll be. If all goes well and you feel comfortable with the prospective roommate, you can then move on to the actual apartment viewing.

As you progress on the decision-making front, you'll need to start talking seriously about the nitty-gritty of day-to-day rooming. Be direct about what you're looking for and answer any of their questions as forthrightly as possible. If you're a total slob, fess up now, and likewise if you're a controlling neat-freak who demands daily vacuuming and semiweekly dusting. Other general issues that you might want to bring up in the course of your gabbing include:

What kind of hours do they keep? If you're a light sleeper, this will be an issue. If you demand regular beauty rest between ten and six, and your potential roomie is nocturnal, it's probably not going to work out for you two.

Do they work fairly regular hours? Will their work take them out of town much? Depending upon what you're looking for in a roommate, these can be important factors. If you want a roomie to keep you from getting lonely, you'll need someone who's going to be around during the same hours that you are. If, on the other hand, you're just looking for someone to help split the costs, then opposite schedules can be dandy, as you'll often have the pad all to your sweet self.

How do they feel about dealing with one another's overnight guests? Do either of you have a significant other that will be spending time over on a regular basis? Will that significant other be contributing to the rent and other shared living costs?

What are their thoughts on how to split chores and bills?

Ultimately, you'll be paying as much attention to the overall feel of your interactions as any of the actual questions and answers exchanged. You want your roommate to be someone you can easily talk to—because if you're finding it hard talking about just the preliminary, getting-to-know-you type fluff, you're going to have a hell of a time bringing up the tough issues once you're actually living together.

Whatever happens, don't make a choice out of desperation. No matter how grim the roommate prospects might seem at the beginning, wait it out till you find someone with whom you can really click—not necessarily as soul mates but on the fundamental issues of sharing a roof.

make it a single: living solo

If you're the sort of person who wants things the way you want them, there's no doubt about it: Solo living's the way to go. No one to monopolize the bathroom when you really, really need to go; no one to clutter up your coffee table with periodicals you have no interest in reading; no one to give

you the evil eye when you don't do the dishes immediately after using them. You can crank up the stereo at one in the morning and dance in the kitchen, in your undies, in the dark—and that's a-okay, because there's no one around for you to answer to except your little old self. You're the only one living under that there roof.

And that's the part that can be a little scary, too.

There are many circumstances under which you might find yourself facing the prospect of living all on your own—and let's be honest now, not all of them are strictly voluntary. Maybe you've moved to a new city where you don't know a soul, and the idea of sharing digs with potential psychopath strangers seems an even bigger risk than setting out solo. Maybe you've been hunting for roommates, but just haven't had any luck. Maybe a brief experience with shared housing has made you realize that you're way too neurotic for anyone else to have to put up with your many, many issues. For whatever the reason, living alone seems to make sense, but you can't quite shake the fear that living with roommates somehow seems easier.

To some extent, you're right: For all that communal living can be a gargantuan pain in the behind, there's something kind of reassuring about knowing that if anything goes wrong in the apartment, you don't have to deal with it alone. Think you hear a noise outside the door? Wake up the roomie and get him to reassure you that you're just imagining things. Toilet's flooding and you don't know what to do while you wait for the superintendent to take his sweet ol' time getting up there to take a look? Run to the roomie for advice . . . or at least commiserate. Even ordinary everyday issues, like making sure the trash gets taken out on time and keeping the house from degenerating into a total slum, become a whole lot more manageable when there's another human or two around to keep your less positive living habits in check. When you're living solo, you have no one to rely on except yourself.

Still, if that's the only thing that's stopping you from stepping into solo life, take the jump. Because the greatest thing about living on your own isn't the decorating freedom or the lack of nagging, but the big self-confidence boost that you get when you realize that you really are fully capable of taking care of yourself.

Money matters are perhaps the biggest factor in determining whether you're really ready to go it solo. Bear in mind that in addition to rent, you'll be shouldering the full burden of telephone, gas, electricity, and water, as well as acting as sole investor in any and all furnishings. Depending on your financial situation, you might find you have to settle for a studio apartment or live farther out from the excitement than you had intended in order to make living alone a feasible reality.

safety first

When you're looking for new digs in a place you plan to live in alone, safety issues become an even bigger priority than usual. Making do with a more modest apartment is fine, but if it means having to live in a very sketchy neighborhood, you might want to rethink your solo living plans and wait till your money situation permits you to live in a place where you don't fear for your life each time you peek out the door.

As you make the rounds on your apartment hunt, pay special attention to how comfortable you'll feel coming home alone, sometimes late at night, to those digs. Visit the neighborhood well after the sun goes down before you commit to calling it home; check to make sure there's good street lighting and take note of how many people seem to be roaming about. Make sure that the entryway, front door, and windows all look secure; ask the landlord or property manager whether it would be possible to get new locks put in before you move in, just to make extra certain that if any old tenants made extra keys, they won't work on your new abode.

For the most part, however, safety precautions are a good idea whether you live alone, or with a bevy of other people. There's no need to get yourself too freaked out about all the things that could go wrong when you're home all by yourself; be smart, be safe, but don't let your paranoia prevent you from enjoying the many pluses of solo life.

the loneliness factor

Of course, some of us just aren't very good at being alone. If you think you'll positively wither away and die if you don't have anyone to talk to after you come home from a long day at work; if you hate reading quietly, watching movies alone, and cooking for no one but yourself; if you can't figure out what to do with yourself during those moments when there's nothing planned for you to do, then being alone probably isn't something that comes naturally to you. But even if you're the deeply social sort who would much rather be hanging with throngs than boring yourself silly sitting at home all by yourself, choosing to live alone might be the best thing ever to happen to you. Learn to enjoy your own company and you'll never find yourself bored again.

Besides, there's nothing to stop you from having people over or getting out there in the great big world whenever you start feeling like too much the recluse, cooped up in your own personal nest. Living alone isn't the same as being alone—except when you want it that way.

shacking up: living with a significant other

So it's been eight months or one year or three and a half or whatever, since you and a certain someone first met in chem lab, at the dining hall, in a bar, wherever, and became a happy twosome. You've seen each other with bed head and kissed each other with morning breath; you've long since stopped keeping track of who pays for what when you go out for dinner or check out a movie; when friends invite one of you over for a party, it's pretty much expected the other one will come along as well. You're madly, head-over-heels in love, and back in college, you pretty much spent every night together at one or the other of your dorm rooms anyway. The financial genius in you starts realizing that you'd be throwing away a lot of money each month paying for two separate places when you'd really only be making full use of one. Maybe, you think, it's time to shack up. Savings incentive aside, there's just one big question looming.

are you really ready?

Unless you're aware that you have commitment issues that have less to do with reality than with your own personal neuroses—and are well on the way to working these out—don't move in with someone until your gut instinct tells you it's right. Moving in together is a big, big step in a relationship, and jumping into it before you're ready is a fabulous way to wreck an otherwise promising thing you've got going.

Yes, there are a multitude of practical reasons why living together might seem sensible. You and your honey might be in the market for new digs at the same time, and it just seems easier to look for one apartment together than to deal with two separate searches. Your current roommate might decide to move in with his girlfriend, leaving you with a spare room to fill, and a significant other who's willing to do so. Still, choosing to live together should be a decision that's based on something more than pure convenience. You might think it a major hassle to kick out a roommate that ends up not working out, but it's nowhere near as excruciating as having to continue to share an apartment with a person you've just broken up with while you wait for one or the other of you to find new digs. Besides, feeling too lazy to put out an ad for a different roommate is not, in and of itself, the strongest basis on which to move your relationship to the next level of commitment. Even if you've spent every night falling asleep in the same bed at one or the other of your places for the past ten months, trust me: It's not the same as actually setting up house as a couple.

For one thing, sharing house means sharing bills—and that means becoming financially tied together in a way that you don't have to when you maintain your own separate residences. Your sweetie's tendency to spend lavish sums might have seemed romantic back in the days when you were just enjoying all the swanky restaurants and pricey gifts, but when you realize that it sometimes means there's not enough money for little things like, oh, rent, you suddenly find yourself turning into the annoying nag who is always chiding about money.

There's also the privacy factor: When you're living together, neither one of you has an obvious place to go during those times when you just want to be alone. Because no matter how crazy about each other you lovebirds are, there will be times when you want to have the freedom to do your own thing, in your own space, with your own friends, on your own time. And that's a healthy thing: The happiest, strongest couples I know are the ones where each half has a solid sense of who they are as individuals, and feels comfortable enough with themselves, and their relationship, to let each other continue to grow. If this is your first grown-up relationship, if neither of you has ever spent any real time apart from each other, if you've only been dating a few months, you might be so wrapped up in the thrill of couplehood that you forget to allow yourselves to explore outside interests, friendships, and adventures. And while that might feel cozy and safe at the beginning, eventually one or the other of you is going to start feeling stifled—all the more so if you're stuck in a cramped one-bedroom apartment where it feels impossible to let out a breath without the other person taking note. Still, as long as you go into the move with a clear understanding that sharing a roof doesn't have to mean losing your individual selves, that good communication is critical, and that compromises will occasionally be necessary, making the transition to living together can make a good relationship even better.

living in sin: dealing with disapproving parents

Sometimes, despite the fact that every fiber in your body tells you that moving in together is the best idea in the world, external forces insist on informing you that you're wrong. When the boy and I first shacked up, we wrote a nice little letter to his grandmother in which we told her about our new two-bedroom apartment. Grammy's reply opened with the following comment: "I was so very glad to hear about your *two* bedroom apartment!" I think she meant it as a joke—or anyway, that's how we chose to interpret it.

Fortunately, Grammy aside perhaps, everybody else in our families seemed to be just fine with the idea of us living in sin. His parents probably would have thought we were crazy to do things any other way. My own parents almost certainly would have felt more comfortable with us doing the wedding thing first, but as immigrants, they'd long since come to terms with the fact that things just worked a little differently in America. But for a lot of people that I've known, family pressures make premarriage cohabitation a whole lot more complicated.

A friend of mine once had a roommate who didn't actually live there. Literally. Each month, this roommate shelled out rent for a space in which she never actually slept. This was just dandy for my friend, as it meant that he had a beautiful and spacious Boston apartment all to himself, at half the cost. Personally, I always thought the roommate was pretty silly—rather than come clean with her parents about the fact that she was living with her boyfriend, she was throwing away a thousand bucks or so a month on an apartment she didn't live in.

Avoidance might seem easier, but ultimately, if you're grown-up enough to be contemplating moving in with a significant other, you're grown-up enough to quit sneaking around behind your parents' backs. Suck up the courage to tell your folks the truth. It's possible they might not be as horrified as you've always imagined and that they'll realize that despite the fact that it's not what they would have chosen for you, you've clearly thought things through and are happy with your decision. And yes, there's also the chance that they'll freak out. At which point, you just have to ask yourself: Can you live with your parents' disapproval, or will it torment you so much that you won't be able to enjoy building your little love nest with the sweets?

If you get the sense that your family cares more about appearances than about you being damned to a fiery afterlife because you're sharing a bed with your significant other, one option is to go for a group housing situation. When there are other roommates around, it's a whole lot easier for parents to delude themselves into believing that you and the sweets are just roommates; certainly, it makes the situation a whole lot easier for them to explain to all the other potentially disapproving aunts and uncles and grandparents and friends. You get to live with your honey without flaunting that fact in your parents' faces—and everyone's happy.

laying down the ground rules

As with any shared rooming situation, communicating clearly from the very beginning about what you both expect out of the living arrangement is key to making sure that you don't end up wanting to throttle one another six months down the line. First and foremost of the issues that you should lay on the table: money. Some of the main financial questions you'll need to discuss up front include:

* Will you be splitting all bills fifty-fifty, or will it be based upon your individual incomes?

* Will one person choose to take care of the electricity and the water, another the telephone and the gas?

* What about shopping for groceries and paying for new furnishings for your digs?

* Will you maintain separate bank accounts, or set up a joint bank account with which to pay for the apartment expenses?

* If you're setting up a joint account, how much will you each contribute from your monthly paycheck, and will you discuss things before buying anything using money from the shared account?

There's no one right answer for how to deal with the financial situation; the thing that's important is to get on the same page.

Of course, making the decision to live together can have some serious implications for the status of your relationship, too. Do you know where you both stand regarding what living together means in terms of commitment? Is this a step on the way to marriage, or is marriage not something you believe in? Don't get all coy about addressing what living together really means for both of you—now is not the time to worry about whether you're going to freak out your partner if you start talking about a long-term shared future.

When you move in together, any final facades have to come down: You see each other exactly as you really are because it's just way too exhausting to be on your best behavior twenty-four/seven. And that's both the good and the bad of it. Because if you're still happy to wake up next to each other every morning despite the fact that his dirty socks piled on the floor drive you crazy or her detached hairs forming an unintentional new rug in your bedroom gross you out, then you know: This relationship is a keeper.

the great apartment search

So you've given it some good serious thought and figured out what you envision for your ideal living situation. If you've decided to go the roommate route and scoured through those Roommate Wanted ads, you may have

scored a new pad and a roomie all in one go. For those flying solo or searching for a love nest, it's time to get started on your next living adventure: the hunt for the perfect pad.

As I write this, I am in dire, dire need of just two simple things: a good pedicure and a livable apartment. For a couple of weeks now, I've been trekking all over the city in search of that ever-elusive perfect apartment for me and the boy, and, as a consequence of all that walking, my feet are a blistered mess.

Way back when, I think I was actually excited about the prospect of scoping out new digs. This was before I actually saw some of the options. See, our hunt for the right pad didn't get off to the most auspicious start. The first place we looked at? It had fossilized pizza chunks adhered to the hallway walls. The ad had boasted hardwood floors, which may or may not have existed under the solid layer of detritus. "We'll get it cleaned up before you move in," the realtor called out hopefully, even as I was trying to inch my way out of the filth without actually touching anything. The one good thing about the experience was that every apartment thereafter looked all right by comparison. Problem was, none seemed exactly right. If it was a nice space, it was in a sketchy neighborhood, or too far from the city center, or located right above a bar; if the location was prime, the apartment was too small, or too dark, or too dingy, or all of the above.

Yeah, apartment hunting can be a massive pain in the behind. Still, as I'm reminding myself every day, all the work's worth it when you finally find a place you love. In the meantime planning, patience, and an open attitude make the whole process just a little bit easier.

when to start looking

Give yourself plenty of time, fellow procrastinators. Finding the right apartment can take a good long while, and remember that ideally, you want your next digs lined up before it's time to clear out of your current space. Two months ahead is not too early.

Or course, timing the apartment search gets a little trickier if you're moving to a new city, as you'll have the whole long-distance thing to contend with. The fuzzy digital photos you might see in an online listing can only tell you so much; even a good picture can be misleading. And it's next to impossible to know where in a city you want to live without actually getting your butt out there and exploring. If possible, try to schedule a trip to your soon-to-be new home city before your intended move. Spend some quality time actually getting to know a little about your new town before you commit to a one-year lease. Take a couple days (or more if you have the luxury) just to explore different potential neighborhoods, taking note of how convenient it is to work, whether there are decent grocery shops and other amenities nearby, and whether you'd feel comfortable walking around the area alone at night. Once you've narrowed down potential areas to focus your search, you can start looking at ads. Ideally, of course, you'll want to be able to view apartments while you're in town. But if there is absolutely no way you can get out there and see a place in person, at least try to see whether you can con a friend or family member in the area into doing some scouting for you. Don't think you know anyone in your future home city? Ask around; it's a small, small, world, and you just might discover that your friend has a friend who can help you out. Even if asking a perfect stranger to check out an apartment for you is just a bit too ballsy, you can at least get a local's opinion on what the general area is like.

how much apartment can you afford?

Unless you're lucky enough to have access to unlimited funds, chances are good that the biggest factor in determining what you'll be looking for in an apartment is budget. The basic rule of thumb for determining how much rent you can afford is to take your monthly salary and divide by three to get your rent. Now, if you're living in a big city, it's entirely possible that the number you get then will be far too puny to secure you anything resembling an actual abode. If you're willing to live very, very frugally in other aspects of your life, and if you don't have a whole lot in the way of loans hanging over your head, you can probably get away with devoting 35–40 percent of your take-home paycheck to housing. If that's still too low to land you a decent pad, you have a few options: 1. Look for apartments that are a little farther away from things. 2. Look for a smaller apartment. 3. Get yourself a roommate.

Where to find out what's for rent. So you kinda have a sense of what you're looking for in your new digs and are ready to begin the hunt. When it comes to actually tracking down apartments that are available for rent, here are a few good places to check out:

Online and newspapers. Local newspapers (and their online incarnations) as well as nationwide apartment listing Web sites (like rent.com, rentnet.com, and apartments.com) are probably the first places you'll look when you begin your apartment search. You might also want to try your local Craigslist.

Brokers. In really tight housing markets, you might find yourself having to turn to the pros for help. A broker basically does the legwork of hunting down potential apartments for you; the small catch is that you have to pay them a substantial fee for their hard labor.

getting prepped to land your apartment

Good things to have when you go apartment hunting:

* A notebook and pen

* A good map

* A checkbook (so you can make the deposit if you decide for certain you want the place)

* Enough money in your bank account to cover a deposit and first month's rent

* Credit report

* Names of references (if you've never rented an apartment before, get character references and a pay stub/tax return/something that proves you have money coming in)

University housing listings. Even if you're not actually a student, universities can be a good source for finding apartments. These days, many university housing offices have online lists as well as information on other resources for finding housing in the area. You can also mosey down onto campus to see if you see any apartment rentals posted on the bulletin boards.

Neighborhood bulletin boards. Coffeeshops, bookstores, record stores, and the like often have handy bulletin boards where people can post their ads; you'll often find "apartment for rent" signs pinned up amid the car-for-sale and massage-therapy ads.

Ride-through/walk-through. If you're dead-set on living in a specific neighborhood, take a morning to explore the area. Grab a notebook and a pen and go on bicycle/foot so you don't have to worry about holding up traffic. Head up and down each and every street of the area in which you're interested as you hunt down FOR RENT signs.

Word of mouth. Tell everyone you know that you're on the hunt for new digs. You never know who might have a lead on a great place that's about to be vacated.

viewing apartments

When you see an ad that looks promising, don't dawdle: Pick up the phone and set up a viewing as soon as possible. In a competitive housing market, apartments go fast. Trust me, there's nothing more disheartening than spending a whole day circling newspaper rental ads, only to find that when you start making calls a day or two later, all the apartments have already been snatched up by folks way more on the ball than you. My boy still occasionally moans about the fabulous river-view apartment we missed out on when we were living in Australia. We let the three Malaysian girls who were at the university housing office at the same time as us use the phone first—which is how they were able to lay claim to the apartment that the boy continues to feel rightfully belonged to us.

The apartment viewing is an interview of sorts—both for you and for your prospective landlord. Show up on time and make an effort not to look like too much of a slob/freak/miscreant. At the same time, bring a notebook and paper along and take the opportunity to ask the landlord whatever questions you might have. A few things you might want to throw out there: How long is the lease for? Is there the option to renew? Are there any additional housing-associated fees besides the rent that you should know about? Are utilities included, and if so, which ones (water, gas, electric)? Does the apartment building have laundry facilities? What's the parking situation? Take note of all the answers, and also get a feel for how well you get along with the landlord and how well they seem like they'd respond to any issues that might come up if you moved into their property.

If a place looks at all like it has potential, take your time to really look it over carefully. Take stock of the closet space and make sure that the door and windows don't look like an easy break-in target. Peek out the windows and check out the views; note the direction they face to get a sense of how much sunlight they're likely to let in (if the windows all face north, for instance, you will pretty much be living in a cave). Make sure that you aren't situated over a bar or a club or anything else that might result in long, sleepless nights spent cursing the noise. If your viewing is during the day, come back to check out the neighborhood at night. Most of all, think about what this apartment would be like if it were filled with your stuff, and how you'd feel coming home to it every day.

Unless you're truly one of the blessed, chances are good that you'll see many, many hideously wrong apartments before you finally stumble across your new home. Try not to get too discouraged as you find yourself traipsing through one dingy place after another, and don't let impatience rush you into settling for something you don't genuinely like. Unless it's obvious that you've been thoroughly unrealistic about the sort of apartment you can get on your budget, it's worth it to hold out for a place you're sure you really like.

on your mark, get set, decorate!

ou've scoured the classifieds, hauled your butt all over town, and finally found an apartment or house that's a happy medium between your itty-bitty budget and those sky-high living dreams. But now, surrounded by four empty walls, a bare floor, and a mountain of un-packed boxes, you suddenly think to yourself: Eek! What next?

Time to start decking out your new digs, of course! Now, maybe you've inherited some odds and ends from the parents and accumulated a few bits and pieces during your college days. But when you look at that chipped dresser you co-opted from your childhood bedroom and the up-side-down box you're using as a night table, you have to admit that some-how, when you were dreaming about living in a place of your very own, this was not what you had in mind. No, what you were hoping for was something just a little more hip twenty-something and a tad less broke college student. With a sigh, you tell yourself you'll just have to settle for now, while college loans, car payments, and credit card debt stand in the way of you and your dream digs.

Yeah, there are a never-ending number of excuses you can make to avoid turning your perfectly adequate but somewhat blah abode into a place that's unequivocally, decidedly, fabulously you. You don't have enough money. You don't have enough time. You don't have any semblance of style. You're waiting till you own, or till you're more settled, or till you're living solo, or with a honey, or till pigs fly. Whatever the rationale, it's time to stop procrastinating. Regardless of where you're at in life, there's absolutely no good reason in the world why you should be living in a pad that doesn't feel like a proper home. Here's how to get yourself motivated and start decorating your digs.

step 1: take stock

When you're surrounded by a mishmash of hand-me-down freebies that are there more for basic function than because you actually gave any thought to whether you liked them, it's hard to imagine how that bland white box of mismatched furnishings is ever going to transform your new digs into a real home. First things first: Once you've made the commitment to start decorating, take a good hard look at what you've already got.

Unless you have a fat wad o' cash burning a hole in your pocket, you'll want to use as much of what you already own as you can. Figure out what furnishings you have that you love, which you can tolerate, and which you positively loathe. The first one's easy to deal with: These are your obvious keepers. As for the second two, well, that's where you'll have to do a little decision-making. A lot of ho-hum or outright hideous furnishings can be rendered mighty dandy with just a fresh coat of paint, some new hardware, a bit of reupholstering, maybe a simple slipcover—in short, a little tender loving care, a small monetary investment, and a free weekend. If the basic bones of a piece of furniture are good, it's probably worth keeping for now. Everything else—the unsalvageably ugly or broken, that is—should be tossed ASAP. Donate it to Goodwill, your little sib's dorm room, wherever, but do whatever you have to do to get rid of the junk. Just because you got it for free doesn't mean you should continue to let it take up space in your house.

Once you've figured out what you have, it's time to think about whether there's anything you'll absolutely need to get in order to render your apartment livable. Now, there are four basic things you'll want to be able to do in your new apartment: snooze, sit, eat, and stash. Which is why Operation Apartment Furnishing will focus on four living fundamentals: a bed, a sofa, a table, and some storage.

snooze . . .

Shortly after graduating from college, my boyfriend and I spent half a year in Australia sleeping on a makeshift bed comprised of two sleeping pads and two sleeping bags wrapped up in a sheet. We saved some money, sure, but we woke up every morning with stiff necks, sore backs, and vile moods. So trust me when I say that if there's one piece of decent-quality furniture you're going to buy, make it a bed, and invest in it ASAP.

If you happen to know someone who has a decent bed they can spare, you're in luck—just haul it away to your new home and you've saved yourself several hundred bucks. But if all you can manage to scrounge up is the tiny twin mattress you slept in as a child, you'll have to go bed-hunting elsewhere. Yes, I know, it's hard to turn down a free bed. But given the fact that most us in our twenties will, from time to time at least, be sharing a sleeping space with another human being, it is my firm belief that anything smaller than a full-size is too cozy for comfort. So ignore the protests of your inner cheapskate for now and start thinking about buying a proper grown-up bed.

For me, at least, there's something just a bit repellent about the idea of sleeping on a complete stranger's used mattress. Thrift store chairs, swap meet tables, flea market bookcases—these I'll take gladly if the condition is good and the price is a steal. But with mattresses, my imagination shifts into paranoia gear, and I can't help but wonder if the previous owner was some filthy slob who liked to roll naked all over the bed, infesting it with all manner of microscopic nasties just waiting for a new host. If you're not as crazy as I am, great: Amble over to some secondhand stores or garage sales and you'll probably find something pretty affordable. But for those of you who are looking in the new market, the options are fewer. Since the traditional box spring/mattress combination is just too posh for tight budgets, that leaves just one solution to the bedding problem: the futon.

Futon mattresses vary widely in quality: The cheap, thin ones may be fine for sofa beds that get limited use, but if you're sleeping on one nightly, it'll have a big ditch in the middle within months. A decent, well-made futon will feel nice and firm and be at least six inches thick. Futons that have a combination of filling and foam tend to offer more support than ones that are just stuffed with loose cotton; for an even better night's sleep, consider one that also boasts springs. Make sure you buy from a store that specializes in quality futons, and ask the salesperson for advice. Then try out any mattresses you're considering by kicking your feet up and giving them a test sleep at the store.

Once you've purchased your futon and set it up in your home, it's best to leave it in its flat position rather than folded up into sofa mode (unless you really need the extra space during the day). Rotate and flip the mattress at least once a month—this will ensure that your mattress stays firm and lump-free, providing night after night of restful beauty sleep—at least until you can afford a real bed.

sit . . .

If you're going to receive guests, you'll need to be able to offer them a comfy seat where they can kick back and relax. Nice, new couches, even from "affordable" furniture stores like IKEA, will still set you back quite a few clams, so chances are slim that you'll be purchasing a sleek new sofa right away.

Here again, the futon may be your best friend. Futons that will be used primarily for sitting need not be as cushy as those used for sleeping, so you'll certainly spend less than you would on a bed. And used sofas don't carry the ick factor associated with used bedding. If you live close enough to a college campus, just wander over there and check out the bulletin boards; chances are good that someone is trying to get rid of his or her futon, and for cheap, particularly in December and May.

You may, however, feel strongly that futon sofas scream "college!" and that your new, sophisticated, grown-up tastes require a genuine, honest-to-goodness couch. Foraging at garage sales, estate sales, and flea markets is a good idea but will probably only turn up functional sofas—tired, ragged pieces faded to some indeterminate shade of gray and undoubtedly riddled with cat hairs. If you are going to go with one of these finds, keep in mind that wood-framed sofas are great, as you can easily make covers to transform that nasty booger-green wool cushion into an elegant gray, a funky orange, or whatever else tickles your fancy.

You mighty also consider looking for a few folding or stacking chairs. These work fabulously in small spaces, as they can be tucked away into a corner or a closet once the guests have departed. Stools are great, too, and can serve as end tables when you don't need them for seating purposes.

eat . . .

If you're working with a small living space, you will probably be quite happy to avoid having to invest in a space-hogging and pricey dining table set. Nonetheless, you'll need some sort of table, primarily to avoid spilling spaghetti all over yourself as you struggle to balance your plate on your lap at mealtimes.

My advice is to look for a coffee table first—to go along with your newly acquired sofa—because chances are good that's where you'll be doing your dining anyway. Decent-looking coffee tables can be found quite easily at garage sales, and for dirt cheap prices. Big trunks also make great coffee tables and have the added advantage of acting double duty as storage.

If you don't like hunching over your coffee table to eat dinner, one option is to sit on the floor and dine Japanese-style. You can buy or make a few small, flat pillows that you can sit on to keep your tush cushioned while you eat. Alternatively, look for folding side/tray tables, which can be stowed away when not in use.

If you're feeling handy, of course, you can also make your own dining table. All you need is a flat surface for the tabletop (a piece of plywood, for instance, which you can find at a place like Home Depot, even a large mirror or piece of glass) and something to support it (wooden stools, low bookshelves . . . whatever you can find for cheap at garage sales and the like). If your tabletop is heavy enough, you won't need to worry too much about it sliding around, as long as you're careful to avoid crashing directly into it. Of course, you can also buy premade table legs and screw them into the top.

stash . . .

Unless you've truly been blessed by the gods of closet space, you will probably find that in your first (miniscule) apartment, built-in storage space is conspicuously lacking. To keep your place under any semblance of order, then, you'll need to come up with some clever ways of storing your belongings.

Your best bet here is to buy used. For clothes, a dresser or wardrobe is traditional, but keep an open mind—anything with compartments will do. At one particularly good estate sale, I managed to snag a very nice solid teak buffet for around $75; sure, it was originally intended for a dining room, but as it happens, it worked great in my bedroom. When shopping for secondhand dressers, look for solid wood rather than cheap fake-wood laminate, as it will hold up much better to abuse and look nicer as well; if the wood surface is dinged up or water stained, you can always paint it. Bear in mind that hideously dated handles and knobs also can be replaced easily with more attractive versions—you can find an exciting array of simple options at most DIY behemoths and hardware stores, or look for fancier ones at home furnishing shops.

While you're out doing your garage sale scouting, keep an eye out for old trunks as well. Big trunks are great for storing off-season clothes, extra blankets, towels, sheets, and more. Even if you don't like the black/dark army green color in which they usually come, you can always give them a paint makeover. Trunks can also be used for table space—in front of your sofa, by your bed, in the hallway, or wherever else you need it.

Once you know what you're actually working with and what you'll have to buy, you're almost ready for the fun part: accumulating! But as you start looking around at coffee tables and sofas and bookcases and more, the possibilities begin to seem overwhelming. You've thought a little about what function you need your furnishings to serve, but now for the hard question: What the heck's your style?

step 2: study up

A friend in college was the first person ever to tell me that I had style. I laughed when she said that. I wasn't entirely sure what she meant, except that as a result, she wanted to drag me on a shopping expedition with her. It was sweet, but I don't think I was much help. After all, I only knew what style worked for *me*.

Style isn't something I think about much. Maybe that sounds strange for someone who runs a home and living zine, but it's the truth. I know *what* I like, but I rarely ponder whether it fits into any neatly defined category of style, and so any attempt to explain my so-called style always leaves me feeling a bit flustered. My home isn't even stylish, at least not in the way I normally think of the word. It's a cozy hodgepodge of stuff I love, stuff my boy loves, and stuff that we merely tolerate because we're still waiting to stumble across the perfect, affordable replacement for said stuff. All of which is to say, *Architectural Digest* won't be calling me up for a photo shoot anytime soon.

Which is just fine by me. My style is about the things that make me happy, not about trying to live up to some magazine's manicured vision of what a beautiful home is supposed to look like. It's quirky, it's mutable, it's evolving, and just about the only thing I can say regarding it, with any amount of certainty, is that with each picture I hang, each lamp I buy, each chair I arrange, I grow more and more confident in the fact that I *know* what I like.

Some days, I'll be flipping through the decorating rags and the inferiority complexes will start plaguing me. But mostly, I think people have it all wrong when they look to books and magazines and interior decorating experts to tell them what colors to use and what tables to buy so they can best achieve that stylish home of some editor's dreams. Stylishness is a matter of being trendy, fashionable, in tune with the latest and the hippest, then adapting your look to suit. Stylishness lacks personality. Having style, on the other hand, is about figuring out what it is that *you* like—pure and simple.

the objects of my affections

For me, style happens in bits and pieces, as I ramble on through life encountering more and more stuff I absolutely must have in my place. Yes, I am a true materialist, and I frequently and obsessively fall in love with objects, big and small. The evolution of my so-called style is, in large part, a history of the objects I have loved. It's not about grand visions or overarching themes but about lamps and bookends and kitchen tools, and a myriad of other mundane, material things that I've amassed over the years.

The object I loved most in my childhood bedroom was a tangerine-shaped white hanging lamp, its crenellated, vaguely alien form the result of some very intricate folding of plastic. It was a weird seventies lamp, which my eighties-hip school friends made fun of relentlessly, but I loved it; when the plastic later became UV-stained and a large section broke off, I begged my parents to find me a new one. That lamp was the first bit of furnishing toward which I ever felt strongly attached, and it amazes me to think that while I caved in to the whims of peer pressure in a zillion other ways, I continued to like that lamp even though my friends found it bizarre. When I finally moved out of my parents' house, my first new apartment splurge was a spherical, white plastic hanging lamp that reminded me of that one from my old bedroom.

The other object that I loved in my parents house was also a seventies-era relic: a little sunshine yellow bookend that essentially consisted of a long piece of metal that was bent at a right angle on one end, then curled up in a springy roll at the other end. The flat side held the books upright, and the coil side snapped snug to hold the books firmly in place. I liked the simplicity of the design—that a single strip of metal could do the job of two traditional bookends; I loved the elegance of its form—from the side it consisted solely of a single circle and a single line; I was completely enamored of the cheery boldness of that yellow hue. I took this particular object with me when I left the familial nest; the little Harvard

So don't worry if you've never before given a thought to whether your tastes run toward art deco or midcentury modern, Japanese minimalist or French provincial. The names, the categories: They don't really matter. But if you haven't a clue as to whether you like furniture simple or ornate, wood or metal, if you're not sure if you prefer warm tones or a cool palette,

Square shop where my parents originally purchased the bookend had long since disappeared, and I couldn't find another like it anywhere. It's a tiny object, so small that it rarely gets noticed, but I can't imagine my place without it.

Sometimes the objects I love are frivolous. One autumn day several years ago, I spied an $86 Alessi "Anna" corkscrew with which I promptly became smitten. It was an adorable anthropomorphic winged corkscrew. The dress was meant to slip around the neck of a wine bottle; you turned her head to screw into the cork, and her arms would slowly rise. Once her arms had reached their maximum height, you'd plunge them back down to her sides; with that one elegant swoop, out popped the cork. (Hmm, as I write this, it's suddenly making me blush.) It was too delightfully clever for words; cute, but this being an Alessi product, still streamlined and chic. I coveted that corkscrew and hinted and hinted about how dearly I wished I could afford my newfound obsession, until come Christmastime, my brother presented me with an Anna of my very own.

Much as I adore that corkscrew, it's still not my favorite object in the kitchen. That honor belongs to a pair of pot holders, hand-quilted by my Mom and given to me for Christmas, just before I moved out to Tucson. There's a navy-blue-edged one and a maroon-edged one, stitched together from a crazy mélange of fabrics, many of which I recognize as remnants from clothing she made for me as a child. They don't match a thing in the rest of my house—I've got a bias toward bold solid colors—but I display them proudly nonetheless. Sometimes the beauty of an object isn't anything external but inherent in less immediately visible factors— who made it, how you acquired it, what it means to you.

A lamp, a bookend, a corkscrew, two pot holders—little things, really, but they're what I think of when I think about my decorating style. It's the objects that have shaped my style—a predilection toward simple lines, an appreciation of clever design, an inordinate fondness for yellow, a weakness for objects with a story—never the other way around, with the style dictating which objects I'll display in my home.

the style file

Start paying attention to what sorts of rooms and furnishings appeal to you when you flip through decorating magazines, go window-shopping at furniture stores, even hang out at friends' pads. Do you like things slightly retro but sleek? Or do you love over-the-top vintage kitsch? Does your taste run toward things modern but classic? Or maybe you like a chic ethnic-inspired look?

Retro

Classic

Ethnic-inspired

Vintage kitsch

even, chances are good that you just haven't done enough looking around yet. Which means before you start buying willy-nilly, it's time to get yourself educated about the options.

Head to the library, your friendly neighborhood chain bookstore monstrosity, or a used bookstore with a good periodicals section. You'll find a dizzying array of magazines devoted to homes and home decorating, featuring page after page of what other people have done to make their pads feel like home. While most of the actual advice you'll find in these tomes is aimed at people for whom a cool $20,000 is a *budget* home makeover, don't despair. The idea here is to learn about what kinds of colors, textures, furnishings, and styles appeal to you. If you're feeling particularly industrious, you might even start keeping a decorating scrapbook; snip out (or photocopy) any decorating pictures that appeal to you, and paste them into a notebook. Eventually, you'll start seeing recurring motifs in what you ooh and aah over. You'll notice that you like round objects, or square objects, or asymmetric objects; that you love anything turquoise, or tangerine, or eggplant; that you have a fondness for stainless steel, or dark-stained wood, or wicker.

Look around at your friends' homes too. Take mental notes concerning what you like about certain pads, and what doesn't work so well for you. When something catches your interest, ask questions—find out where your friend got that cool table lamp, or how they made that funky coffee table. Most people love talking about what they've done with their nests, so you'll earn extra brownie points for actually noticing their décor and pick up a few tips you might be able to crib for your own place as well.

Inspiration can come from less obvious sources as well—a hike in the mountains in autumn, that backpacking trip in Italy, a prized collection of vintage postcards, a stop at that florist shop just around the corner from your apartment. Color, especially, is everywhere you turn, and once you make a point to start noticing it all around, you'll find you rapidly get a sense of which colors make you the happiest, or give you the greatest sense of calm, or get you the most energized.

Whatever you do, avoid limiting yourself to thinking you have to copy one specific style. My favorite homes are the ones where the décor can't be reduced to one neat description, but show as much quirkiness as the fine folks who live there. Ultimately, style is as much about confidence as it is about aesthetics. Take a little time to explore the options, and learn to listen to your gut instincts. Trust yourself to know that this lamp is fabulously you, and that chair is decidedly not, and slowly, the little pieces of your very own unique style will start to fall into place.

step 3: one step at a time

So you're beginning to get a sense of what you might like to do with your space. Still, there's the image you have of your dream pad in your head, and the reality of what you're actually living with in the right here right now. And getting from here to there seems, well, nigh impossible. When you think of it as one grand task, decorating can seem hopelessly daunting.

The key is to think of decorating as a gradual evolution, rather than an all-at-once transformation. Unless you have astounding powers of sorcery at your disposal, you are not going to turn your dormesque living room into a swinging lounge in one weekend. But you can change the color scheme by whipping together some new throw pillow covers, or thrift-shop for a new coffee table, or frame some artwork for the walls—little changes that can make a big difference in bringing your pad one step closer to cool. Breaking up the decorating process into a series of much smaller projects makes the job seem infinitely more feasible and at the same time provides a much more wallet-friendly approach to the overall task at hand, as it allows you to attend to each minitask as time and budget allow.

So grab a pen and paper and make a list of everything you want to make, everything you want to revamp, everything you want to buy. Don't censor yourself: Dream as big as you want. Getting practical comes later. This is your decorating to-do list, and once you feel you've pretty much got everything covered that'll need to happen in order to create your stylin' new digs, it's time to prioritize. Divide the tasks into three categories: short-term to do, middle-term to do, and long-term to do. On the short end of the spectrum, list the quick, the cheap, the easy—anything that can be accomplished with a minimum of effort and/or money. You'll also list the essentials here, like a bed, that might eat a more substantial chunk of your bank account than other things, but that you really can't go all that long without. At the longer end of the to-do spectrum, you'll be including projects that may take you a good long while before you can find the moolah or the free time to attend to the task and that aren't strictly crucial to your survival.

Start with the quickie projects first and you'll soon find that you're making clear progress toward your decorating goals. Cross them off as you go—it's fun! It's satisfying! And it'll make you feel mighty proud. Pretty soon, you'll look around one day and realize that though your home is not quite perfect, it's looking quite nice nonetheless—and getting closer to feeling like the digs of your dreams all the time.

the real deal

year after I graduated from college, I found myself sharing my very first real apartment with my boyfriend. We were living in a little city in edge-of-nowhere Australia—about as far from our home state of Massachusetts as you could possibly get, and still be on the planet Earth, that is. The rent was cheap, and the location convenient to the school where we'd be studying during our one-year stint abroad—at least, those were the rational reasons we told ourselves for choosing our place. Mostly, though, I suspect we'd picked the bland two-bedroom town house because it featured a pool. What we failed to factor into the "good" rent price was that the apartment, like most, came completely unfurnished. We moved in with just two suitcases, a duffel bag, and a hiking backpack—and found ourselves faced with a big, vaguely eighties-esque pastel box that featured a whole lot of empty space between its long, bare walls. The few measly bits of furniture we'd acquired in our college dorm days remained back at home in our parents' basements. For the next twelve months, we had this place to call our own, and we were starting completely from scratch when it came to the furnishings department.

With phone bills, electric bills, water bills, and the monthly rent suddenly plaguing us on a regular basis, plus food and car eating up another substantial chunk of our bank accounts, the frugal side of our Yankee roots soon reared its head as we realized we'd have to supply our apartment with at least the bare necessities. This, then, is the only reason I can give for how I came to spend five months of my life sleeping on two inflatable camping pads, fluffed up by a layer of sleeping bags, loosely bound together by a fitted sheet. What started off seeming (rather sensibly) like a home essential soon dropped rank in our priority list as we realized that a good new mattress would set us back a fair amount of cash, and that the idea of sleeping on one of those dingy used beds I'd seen at the thrift store placed just shy of wearing secondhand underwear on my personal gross scale. Many backaches and restless nights later, we finally sucked it up and bought ourselves a mattress. Only now, instead of getting a whole year's worth of comfortable sleep out of our investment, we'd only be enjoying half that time before we'd have to sell it off and move on back to the States.

That little experience taught me some important lessons. One: Never underestimate the value of a good night's sleep. And two: There's a big difference between being sensibly frugal and just plain being a cheapskate.

When you're moving into your first real quasi-adult home and trying to deck it out on a less-than-lavish budget, it's just as easy to fall into the trap of being overly stingy with your spending as it is to launch a shopping spree that will leave you financially hurting for a long time after the adrenaline rush of consumerism wears off. As with most things in life, the ideal approach lies somewhere in the middle.

your needs versus your wants

So you're decking out your first digs and shopping at your favorite fun-design-at-cheap-prices store, and naturally, you find yourself oohing and ahhing over all the absolutely adorable whatsits and doodads that catch your eye at every turn. Though you'd headed off in search of some simple and much-needed bookshelves, you come home instead with a trunk full of whimsical striped vases, lamps shaped like flowers, kitchen accessories that look like abstracted smiley faces and aliens and animals. Meanwhile, as you're happily admiring all your new purchases, you find that you still don't have anywhere to put all those books that are sitting in boxes in the middle of your living room.

Don't get me wrong: I'm all for injecting plenty of personality into the decorating process. But when you're really on a budget, it pays to just stop and ponder a bit before you make too many of those impulse buys. Before you shell out the dough for something you think you really want but know you don't really need, ask yourself a few simple questions:

1. Can you make something similar for a whole lot less moolah, and would it be worth your effort to do so?

2. If the answer is no, do you have the money for this? (And by "have," I don't just mean that your credit card limit will cover the sum.)

3. If you spend the money on this, will it mean you won't have enough to buy something else that's going to give you a whole lot more use?

4. If the answer to number three is yes, will it really, truly make up for that in enjoyment alone?

Think hard, and be brutally honest with yourself. Make a list of everything you think you'd like to have for your ideal apartment and prioritize based upon how essential the item truly is to your home comfort. Make sure you have the funds to cover the basics before you start spending willy-nilly on the frills. Generally, you'll find that it's a lot easier to figure out a no- or low-budget way to accessorize than it is to scare up a good mattress with little money.

go for value, not just price

Getting a good deal isn't always about doling out the least amount of cash. That $300 new sofa might seem like a fab price when you compare it to the usual $800 plus that most furniture stores will ask for what looks like the same, but chances are good that the budget version's not just cheap, but cheaply made. It might look great and feel okay for a year, maybe two or three if you're lucky, but before you know it, the cushions will be sagging or the upholstery will be coming apart at the seams, or worse, the frame will suddenly decide to call it quits. And you'll be back where you started, shopping for another couch.

There are times when you'll do just fine to go with the lowest-priced option, but when it comes to items that will be getting a lot of use, you will generally find it's much wiser to spend a little more to get the better-made product. For most folks, that'll mean the bed and the sofa, major appliances, and electronics—higher-ticket items that can last you a good long while when they're solidly crafted, and cause you a fair amount of headache when they're not.

time is money, too

Price and quality are key in the overall value equation, but there's a third factor that you have to take into account as well: time. As much as I get a kick out of scoring a really sweet price on a purchase, I've never understood folks who will drive miles out of their way just to get the gas that's a mere penny cheaper per gallon or run around to five different supermarkets to gather their groceries in order to get the very lowest prices possible on each item on their shopping list. Bargain hunting inevitably involves an investment of time, and at a certain point, the amount of money you save just isn't made up by the number of hours you have to put in to do so. Don't let your cheapskate urges lead you into wasting the undoubtedly precious amount of free time you happen to have. If you find yourself faced with a dining table set that you adore that offers decent value for its price tag and that you can reasonably afford, quit vacillating and just go for it.

Essentially essential or why I bought a painting when I needed a couch. One Saturday, while on a weekend getaway to celebrate our first wedding anniversary, my boy and I fell in love at first sight. Not with each other—that falling happened long, long ago, and after many, many sights—but with a gorgeous eight-and-a-half-foot-tall beauty that we spied while wandering aimlessly, innocently through the small shops and tiny galleries of Bisbee, Arizona. This particular beauty happened to be hanging proudly on the tall white walls of a gallery just off the main drag. It was a big, bold, mixed-media diptych entitled *Urban Cowgirls,* by a local artist named William Spencer III. It was beautiful, and enigmatic, and fascinating—a total surprise—and when we saw it we just had to stop and stare.

Bisbee, a lovingly restored old copper mining town nestled in the mountains of southern Arizona, is quaint and charming, full of infectiously friendly local townsfolk who are quite obviously very content to be living where they are, and seemingly happy to share their town with the many weekend tourists as well. It is a very pleasant place to be, but it is not the sort of place I visit expecting to buy anything substantial. The antique shops are fun but overpriced; the galleries are affordable but largely unimpressive. There are plenty of things sold as art here, sure, but it's largely of the cheesy Southwest, pastel-earth-tones, cacti- and cowboys- and Indians-themed variety. We were not expecting to find any art there that we liked; we were certainly not in Bisbee to buy art.

Poor twenty-somethings that we are, the boy and I aren't much in the habit of ever buying art really, preferring, instead, to populate our walls with things priced to suit our miniscule budget. That by and large means free, like my photographs and his textural-art projects, and miscellaneous other lovely things made and gifted to us by people we know. This method has worked well for us: Our walls are jam-packed with neat stuff to look at. We've been lucky enough to avoid Bare Wall Syndrome, that most common of young apartment dweller maladies. We have more artwork than we have wall space. We do not, in short, need more art.

But when we saw this painting we knew we deeply, desperately wanted to bring it home. It wasn't quite need, but it was one of those wants that feels pretty close. There were other works in the gallery that we found perfectly pretty—some by the same artist, another by a different one—and that in itself was astounding, that amid all the dreck we'd seen that day, this one gallery space had not one but several pieces we rather liked. But *Urban Cowgirls* was the one we kept coming back to, circling round and round the gallery only to return to the same spot each time. We loved its rich reds and soothing blues and greens, its layer upon layer of texture, its intriguingly abstracted geometric shapes jutting this way and that way in a funkily rhythmic composition that seemed chaotic at first, then felt perfectly, artfully balanced the longer we looked at it. But a quick glance at the price tag promptly squashed any fantasies we'd been entertaining about owning it. We left the gallery that first day feeling sad that some lucky rich bastard, undoubtedly less deserving, would no doubt snatch up that diptych that we loved so much—for some stupid, shallow reason no doubt, like it matched his sofa or something.

After dinner that night, we couldn't help but take a stroll past the gallery again. And by "couldn't help," of course, I mean "walked in the complete opposite direction of where our car was parked." It was late and the gallery was closed, but through the windows, by the faint glow of the streetlights, we could see the diptych still hanging there. The more we thought about it, the more the circles in the painting looked like traffic lights, or rotaries, or cul-de-sacs; or maybe parts of factories; the black-and-white striped paths like pedestrian crosswalks perhaps. Juxtaposed against the silk-screened cowgirls sitting tall in their saddles along the bottom of the piece, it seemed the quintessential modern Southwest piece, a sly comment on the way that urban/suburban sprawl is so rapidly consuming the character that once defined the Wild West. With faces pressed up close to the gallery window, we stared, talked, and overanalyzed our new favorite painting. Then we played the what-if game, and the funny thing was that the more we talked about it, the more possible it seemed.

It is a scary, scary thing to plunk down any significant amount of money, but it's scarier still when you're spending it on something as ostensibly "impractical" as art. It's not like buying a house, or a car, or splurging on a luxurious bed; art doesn't shelter you from the elements, or get you where you need to go, or make it easier for you to get a good night's rest. It doesn't do much of anything, really; it has no function, no utility, no practical reason for taking up the space it takes. We went back and forth, mulling over the pros and cons of whether we would be spending frivolously. The painting was expensive (by our standards); it was huge; it would really look much better in the sort of a grand, spacious loft that we would probably never be able to afford. With the same amount of money, we could buy the long-coveted real sofa to replace the hand-me-down futon we'd been complaining about for three years now.

But what it comes down to is that in the end love, alas, is not rational. A good sofa we could find anywhere, anytime, but the perfect painting is a much more elusive find. We looked at each other and knew we'd be returning the next day, checkbook in hand.

A painting may not be as functional as a sofa, but in this house at least, it delivers just as much satisfaction. These days, I'm still sitting on a lumpy, bumpy, sore-back-inducing old futon sofa when I watch TV. But when my sweetie and I are in the kitchen each evening, sharing dinner, we look up at our fabulous, marvelous one-of-a-kind painting and can't help but grin.

In the end, the real worth of an item isn't in its dollar amount, but in how much satisfaction it ultimately gives you. Balance your head sense with your heart sense, and every investment that you put into your new digs—no matter how big or small—is sure to feel like a real deal.

Still, while this is all well and good, where the heck's a newbie apartment dweller to turn in search of that ideal combination of quality, style, and value? Shop at regular retailers and you'll generally just have to settle for two out of three. If it's well made and gorgeous, it won't be cheap; if it's sturdy and cheap, it won't be pretty; if it's cheap and adorable, it'll be programmed to self-destruct. No, if you're looking for goods that work well, look cool, and cost little, there's really only one reliable route to go: secondhand.

secrets of a secondhand shopaholic

I was a teenage mallrat. Or I would have been, had not the music lessons, Chinese school, and art classes put a limit on my spare time. When my cousins—my favorite partners in budding consumerism—and I would beg our parents to drop us off at the mall on those rare free weekend afternoons, my uncle would look at us with disdain and declare: "Shopping's just a waste. If you buy something, you're wasting money; if don't, you're

wasting time." Though I eventually came to see the light of his wisdom when it came to whiling away hours of my time trying and buying such nonnecessities as stirrup pants and purple mascara (actually, as hindsight shows, run-away-in-horror-screaming antinecessities). I have to admit that I've never quite kicked the shopping habit. I like stuff, and I have the jam-packed house to prove it.

We're living in a material world, baby, and I am a material girl—but fortunately for my bank account, I'm a much smarter shopper than I used to be. My purchases are informed more by what I can afford (generally not a whole lot, alas) and what I know I really love, than by the latest fashions featured in *Seventeen* magazine. This is a good thing. These days, I visit the mall only about once a season. But on weekends, you'll frequently still find me shopping—working the secondhand thang all around town.

Back when I was thirteen, the phrase, "What, did you get that at Betty's?"—delivered with a snootily adolescent sneer—was the biggest put-down you could possibly bestow on anyone. Betty's, as everyone in the whole school knew, meant Betty's Thrift Shop, the one and only second-hand boutique in my small suburban Boston town, and heaven help your standings in the eighth-grade social hierarchy if anyone ever spied you actually walking into or out of its ramshackle little brown door. If anyone had ever dared suggest back then that I would one day scour moving sales and estate sales, Salvation Armies and Goodwills and, yes, even dank and musty little places just like Betty's, I would have shuddered in revulsion and publicly proclaimed my disgust for all things less than shiny and new. Funny what a difference a decade (okay, plus some) can make. Most Saturday and Sunday mornings these days, you can find the boy and me tooling around all over town, hopping from estate sale to moving sale, then making a final pit stop at our favorite thrift store. I've wholeheartedly embraced the Church of the Secondhand Shopper, and like all religious converts, I preach its teachings with zeal.

Buying secondhand is time-consuming, frustrating, and utterly, undeniably addictive. It's also the best way to get those apartment necessities—sofa, tables, bookshelves, lamps—without completing depleting your bank account. But how do you break into the world of secondhand goods? A few general tips for those beginning the bargain hunt:

Shop often. Be patient. Okay, let's take a trip back to your college intro psych class. Remember the poor lab mouse who would keep pressing that stupid lever, hoping against all hope that this time he'd hit gustatory gold and get that little food pellet, this despite the fact that his efforts frequently yielded *nada*? The seductive allure of thrifting is a textbook-perfect example of the partial reinforcement effect: Most days you'll find nothing, but just when you're about to give up and renounce flea markets and yard sales as a complete waste of time, you'll unearth a great deal that'll convince you that maybe, just maybe, you're not quite ready to quit cold turkey. Needless to say, if you're looking to furnish your home primarily through secondhand sources, you're going to need to have a lot of time and heaps of patience.

Stay open-minded. Barring a divine miracle, you will not find *exactly* what you're looking for. If you've got your heart set on a sleek gray sofa just like the one you saw in your IKEA catalogue, you're best off skedaddling on over to the nearest store and plunking down the cash. If, on the other hand, you're just looking for anything suitable for lounging about, you'll have a much greater chance of succeeding via the secondhand route. Remember that wood and metal can always be repainted, ugly fabric remedied with a slipcover or new upholstery, and that there's no reason in the world that an object needs to be put to its original conventionally intended use.

On the other hand, know your decorating style. The difference between a college dorm room furnished entirely in used goods and a quasi-adult apartment done floor-to-ceiling in secondhand is simple: a sense of style. Namely, the fact that the former lacks it. Cultivate your own distinct look for your home, be it contemporary minimalist, retro space age, wildly kitsch, rustic charm, or whatever. Even if the desired effect is your personal brand of eclectic, it'll never work unless you make a conscious effort to buy only items that genuinely suit you. I don't care how good of a deal those dining chairs might be; if the only thing they have going for them is their low price, keep on shopping.

Bring plenty of cash. Plus a checkbook for backup. At flea markets and yard sales, you'll have better bargaining power if you can pay in cash. But just in case you stumble across the perfect vintage armchair and it's just slightly more than what you've got in your wallet, you'll want to have your checkbook handy so that you can snatch up your find before someone else makes off with it.

Suggested furniture-thrifting toolkit: plenty of strong rope, bungy cords, a thick blanket or two, screwdriver/swiss army knife, and a strong friend. If you're looking for furniture, you'll want to make sure you can actually cart your sofa (table, entertainment unit, whatever) away once you find it. One of the downsides of buying large items secondhand is that delivery is just not an option. If you've got a truck, you're set. For those of us who aren't blessed with gas-guzzling behemoths for vehicles, however, you'll need ropes and bungy cords to secure your purchases to the roof, or to keep your back trunk—which inevitably will be just an inch too short or deep to fully accommodate your acquisition—from popping open when you drive. Blankets make fine furniture pads. Use them to prevent both your furniture and your car from getting all scratched up.

Get rid of the old old to make room for the new old. Because once you start doing the secondhand thing you'll find it almost impossible to stop—it's just so damn exciting when you find something terrific for next-to-nothing—you'll soon find yourself buying things even when you don't really need them. The only way to prevent your house from becoming a teeming mass of junk is to conquer those pack-rat tendencies and learn to weed. Donate the ugly, the broken, and the useless to Goodwill. Or perpetuate the cycle by having a garage sale of your own.

Secondhand shopping comes in a wide range of formats, from quaint antique marts to dingy charity-run thrift stores, tiny consignment shops to ginormous weekend flea markets, neighborhood yard sales to online auctions. Here's a beginner's guide on how to make the most of our favorite secondhand sources.

how to thrift-store

Charity-affiliated thrift shops offer the cheapest goods and the widest selection. The reason for this is simple: Most of the goods that places like Goodwill, the Salvation Army, and other charities are hawking were donated, so they can afford to sell stuff for dirt cheap and still make a tidy little sum.

There's a fine art to thrift-store shopping. It takes a good eye, an ability to turn on the blinders to the vast amount of junk you'll inevitably encounter on your excursions, and a heap of patience. It's not the quickest or the easiest path toward an abode filled and furnished with all your little heart has ever desired. But for the quasi-adult on a tight budget, thrift stores are one of the best places you can go to discover great stuff at prices that are just short of a steal. They're also fantastic sources for creative decorating inspiration, as you never know what wacky and wonderful style of good you're going to unearth on any given thrift-shopping venture.

The big nationwide thrift stores like Salvation Army, Goodwill, Value Village, and (my personal favorite) Savers generally have lots and lots of stuff, but the problem with these places is that every thrift store treasure-hunter in town is probably riffling through the same inventory. Check out some of the lesser-known, locally run thrift stores in town as well—they'll almost certainly have a smaller selection, but when you do make that fabulous rare find, it'll probably be at a real bargain. One of my best thrift store scores was a big, white sixties space-age-style fiberglass coffee table that I snatched up for a mere $20 at a tiny, out-of-the-way thrift shop run by a small local charity. The table had apparently been sitting there for weeks, just waiting for my boy and me to stumble across it. You can bet that at a better-trafficked store, some other sixties-loving hipster would have snatched that table long before we'd ever chanced upon it.

Good home stuff to look for when you're thrift-store shopping. Here's what to look for when you're hitting the thrift stores:

Fabric. Sheets, tablecloths, drapery, even clothing (provided it's not something you'd feel bad tearing into) are all excellent, cheap sources for funky material that you can use for making pillow covers and slip-covers, reupholstering, or whipping up some window treatments. If you find random bits of pretty patterned fabric that you adore, but for which you can't find any practical use, pop them into frames for instant wall art, or stretch them across basic wood frames like a canvas painting.

Furniture. Thrift stores offer plenty of super-cheap furniture options for the impecunious quasi-adult decorator. But it pays to know what you're getting a good deal on, and what's just ugly, rickety, possibly infested crapola that's not even worth the time and effort it would take you to drag it back home. High on my list of furniture to steer clear of at thrift stores: sofas. Really, I'm not a particularly fussy sort when it comes to worrying about grime, dust, even germs when buying secondhand—pro-vided the item in question can be easily and thoroughly cleansed, that is. But anything big, upholstered, and likely to have had pets lounging on it for significant amounts of time in its history . . . well, let's just say that having had one very itchy experience with a flea-ridden, thrift-shop-purchased sofa a few years back, I've learned my lesson. If you can't see the home where the sofa came from, be very, very wary. If, after carefully weighing the matter, you choose to take the gamble of schlepping the sofa back home, well, you've been forewarned. At the very least, give it a good flea-ridding and thorough steam-cleaning be-fore you decide to take your first nap on it.

Still, there's plenty of other furniture that you should definitely keep an eye out for while browsing the thrift stores. Tables, dining chairs, bookshelves, and the like are a much safer bet than sofas. They'll gener-ally look pretty nasty if they've made their way into a thrift store—peel-ing paint, beat-up finish—but most cosmetic flaws can be quickly and cheaply remedied with a can of paint and a couple hours of time.

Lamps. I have a deep, irrational love for nifty lamps—to the point where I now have several sitting in the garage unused because I don't have anywhere else in the house that really needs yet another source of decorative lighting—and thrift stores are one of my favorite places to find them. You can find lamps with beautiful, unusual shapes that just need a little spray paint, a new shade, and some easy rewiring work perhaps.

Picture frames. If you're really lucky, you might even find a whole picture that's worth adding to your décor—but for the most part, the "art" found in thrift stores is only of interest if you're going for the "so bad it's good" kitsch factor. But the frames around said art are often in fine condition, and thrift stores often have empty frames as well. You can replace broken Plexiglas by getting new sheets cut to size, and paint frames to suit your fancy.

Containers. Glass jars, metal tins, baskets . . . thrift stores offer all sorts of stuff that's good to help you get your odds and ends organized.

Glassware. Looking for wineglasses for your next dinner party? Shot glasses, old-fashioneds, maybe some martini glasses for your next soiree? Then hop over to your favorite thrift store—if you're willing to forego the matchy-matchy set and go with the eclectic style instead, it's the best way to get real glassware cheaply.

Old records and record albums. The records in your average thrift store are generally in such a sad state that they're no longer good for their original use. But they're just perfect for home decorating purposes. Make a record bowl, turn a hilarious collection of wacky album covers into wall art, or make a funky storage box with album covers.

Don't be dismayed when you wander into a thrift store for the first time and there's just junk, junk, junk everywhere. The plethora of dusty, dirty, decrepit goods can easily make the few quality goods in the store look crappy as well. Ignore the chaos. Two important things to remember: 1. Anything worth buying will look a thousand times better in your clean, attractive apartment than it will in the dingy store. 2. A quick cleaning and a new coat of paint can work miracles. Of course, even paint can't transform something that's cruddily made into a sturdy piece of furniture. Don't buy crap. In many ways, thrift-store shopping isn't any different than buying new: You're looking for good value, and that means making sure you're getting the most for your time and money.

how to estate-sale

Yard sales, garage sales, flea markets, rummage sales, Goodwill, Salvation Army, and the like are all fine sources for snagging secondhand goods at rock-bottom prices, but when it comes to finding the real treasures, nothing beats an estate sale. Just about every truly cool, remotely valuable bit of furnishing I have in my home was purchased at an estate sale—that teak dining table set with the beautiful curved-back wood chairs, our funky vintage orb lamp, the sleek mid-century-modern walnut daybed. For anyone with high-end tastes and low-end budgets, estates sales are just pure shopping heaven. True, what begins as a perfectly sensible, very smart way to furnish your digs cheaply may eventually turn into the sort of can't-live-without-the-fix addiction that sends you scurrying to find a support group to wean you off that irresistible estate sale high. But when you've finally reached the stage of life when your parents' ratty hand-me-down futon and the coffee table you salvaged from a Dumpster no longer seem like appropriate furniture for someone with your fine sense of style, estate sales are the way to go. In fact, there's only one real drawback of estate sale shopping: The elderly love 'em, so be prepared to do battle with all little old ladies who won't hesitate to push you out of the way to get to the Hummel collection.

So what the heck's an estate sale, anyway? Estate sales stand apart from your regular old, garden-variety yard sales/garage sales in that they occur after a person has passed away. Now, if you're first reaction to that is "Ewwwww, that seems a little morbid," trust me, I understand. The first time I ever stumbled upon an estate sale, I have to admit: It did weird me out a little to realize that all of us bargain-hunters were fighting over some poor old dead person's things like vultures circling around a roadkill. But what I've realized now is that while death is sad, estate sales actually serve to make a very difficult time for the surviving family just a tiny bit easier, by saving them the hassle of figuring out just what they're going to do with all the stuff that they can't use themselves.

Generally, the entire contents of the deceased's home are offered for sale, and when you show up at the house, you'll be allowed to wander around from room to room to peruse the goods. An estate sale isn't an auction (although estate auctions exist as well)—you'll find a price sticker (or sign) on everything that's for sale, although you should feel free to try politely bargaining those prices down, if you're so inclined to do that sort of thing. Sometimes the family of the deceased will run the estate sales themselves, but the best ones, I've found, are organized by professional estate sale companies that generally only agree to take on an estate if they believe the goods are plentiful enough, and of high enough quality, that a weekend sale will generate them a heap of moolah.

How to find an estate sale. Estate sale listings can be found in the classified section of the newspaper, generally under "Yard Sales/Garage Sales," or, as is the case with my city's paper, under a separate section specifically devoted to auctions and estate sales. Look in the Friday and Saturday editions of your local newspapers to find the weekend's offerings. Or save yourself the quarters and peruse the classifieds online.

When to go. If you're looking for something specific, especially a larger item like a dining table, sofa, or the like, it's best to show up as early as possible, since these are the sort of items that tend to disappear quicker than you can whine, "Seven A.M. is an ungodly hour of the morning to have to wake up on a Saturday morning!" Which may be completely true, but rest assured that if you decide to sleep in and catch up on just a few more hours of your beauty rest, you'll discover that everything useful—and in good condition—will have a big fat SOLD sticker slapped across its price tag.

If an estate sale ad says the sale starts at eight A.M., you should ideally get there at five minutes to eight (anything earlier is, frankly, just plain obnoxious), or more realistically and at the very latest, by nine o'clock. Wait any longer and that set of solid-hardwood bookcases that you've been coveting for months now will almost certainly have disappeared.

On the other hand, if you just have a bit of time to kill and like to browse estate sales for the pure fun of the experience, the best deals are generally found on the last day of a weekend-long sale, or in the afternoon of a one-day-only sale. In those final desperate hours before a sale is set to end, the sellers will frequently announce that everything remaining is 50 percent off the marked price. This is when you'll find the real bargains—though be aware that you may find yourself hauling back all manner of items that you never before thought you actually needed—a bowling ball, a Buddha lamp, a strobe light, an Elvis ashtray, a croquet set.

Be prepared. First and foremost, you'll need a good map of the city. Professionally run estate sales usually provide excellent directions in their ads, plus very clear signs once you get close to the treasure trove, but privately held estate sales can be more difficult to actually locate without the aid of a map. After you've filtered out the most promising estate sales from the classifieds, write down all the addresses and look them up on a map, then plan out the most sensible and efficient route to take.

Don't leave the house without your checkbook in hand—cash is great, and may even give you better bargaining power, but unless you normally walk around with two hundred bucks in your back pocket, you'll need the checks to be able to pay for the big items. Also, if you think there's a chance that you may be buying anything large, bring along plenty of rope, bungee cords, and a blanket or two, so that you can strap your finds to the top of your car. If you do end up stumbling across the cherry buffet table of your dreams, however, and just can't find any way to lug it home in, say, your VW bug, no worries—just ask the sellers if you can pay for it now and return later to pick it up. Then rush home and call up your buddy—the one with the mammoth pickup truck, of course—for a little favor.

how to e-thrift

Of course, schlepping yourself around from one thrift store to another can get exhausting. If you're looking for a specific little something for your humble abode, scouring online for a good secondhand deal can save you a whole lot of time and energy.

As you start your online hunt for those new-to-you goods, check out the following Web sites.

Freecycle.org. Freecycle is made of individual communities based in cities all over the United States and around the world. The concept is pretty simple: Members can post about items they're getting rid of, as well as items they're seeking. The best part—every item listed has to be 100 percent free, with the only catch being that you generally have to scuttle your behind over to fetch your score in person. If the skeptic in you thinks this means that the only things you'd be able to get through freecycle are unusable junk, think again. Folks are consistently downsizing, upgrading, and moving house, and when the thought of trying to organize a garage sale is just way too stressful, they'll turn to fellow freecyclers to help make their lives a little easier by carting their unneeded stuff out of sight. You can find dining table sets and sofas, end tables and lamps, throw pillows and rugs, and more. And should you grow tired of any of these goods, you can always send them back into the freecyclin' world from whence they came.

Craigslist.org. Like Freecycle, Craiglist is based upon individual communities organized by city; unlike Freecycle, most of the goods you'll see listed are going to cost you a little something. Still, most ads are posted by regular folks just looking to get rid of their stuff rather than make a big profit, which means you can get some great deals on all sorts of furnishings.

eBay.com. Unless you've been living in a cave for the past five years, you already know about eBay. Sadly, eBay is probably a big part of the reason it isn't as easy to get a really sweet deal on genuine vintage design as it used to be, as the actual value of these finds is now readily accessible to any schmo who knows how to use a search engine. And anyone who is bidding or selling on eBay is Internet-savvy enough that they've already Googled how much that Eames chair they found in their dearly departed great-aunt's house is really worth. Still, the sheer volume of goods on offer at the online auction behemoth makes eBay well worth a peek. If you can't find it on eBay, it probably doesn't exist.

Check listings often, and if you see something you're interested in, get in contact with the seller right away with whatever questions you might have. Get details about both the aesthetic and working conditions, how old the item is, what the dimensions are—all the key questions that'll affect whether this item is right for you. If it's a geographical impossibility for you to check out an item in person, ask for photographs, preferably taken from a variety of angles. If the seller is too lazy to furnish you with any, keep moseying.

Once you've spied something that looks promising, make sure that the goods can get to you, or vice versa. Check to see where the seller is based, and whether the item you're interested in can be either delivered or picked up in person. For items to be delivered, find out about shipping and handling charges before you bid or buy, as they can sometimes be ridiculously high.

Buying stuff you've never seen from people you've never met, and through a venue that doesn't actually physically exist, can be a scary thing. And yeah, sadly, there are some mean, bad people out there who have no problem whatsoever with taking your money without ever giving you what was promised. Still, most sellers out there are perfectly legit—and probably just as wary about your potential sketchiness as you are of theirs.

So shop responsibly. If you're buying through eBay, for instance, check the seller's ratings and feedback before you bid. And no matter what the venue, buying with Paypal or a credit card is fine, and if it turns out the seller is a scam artist, you can always file a claim. If you're transacting person-to-person and worried about potential stalkers and other scary folk, bring a friend with you when you go to retrieve your goods; if the item in question is relatively small, meet up at a local coffeeshop or other neutral, public location. Of course, as the buyer, you also have the responsibility to be considerate of your seller. As soon as you and the seller have agreed that you're the lucky winner of whatever, pay promptly. And if your new goodie needs to be picked up in person, make arrangements to do so in a reasonable amount of time—and stick to the agreed-upon date and time.

If you get your item and find it's been damaged, or that the item's condition has been misrepresented, contact the seller right away. Be polite, as very few people in the world react well to rude, angry e-mails or phone calls, and don't file a negative public review for all the world to see before talking with the seller one on one. If playing nice doesn't get you anywhere, go for persistence. Write additional e-mails or letters, make phone calls, let the seller know you'll be reporting them to whatever community you bought from—get pushy. Most bad sellers aren't trying to scam you, they're just lazy, and if you bug them long enough, you'll likely end up getting what you want.

to buy or not to buy . . . ah, the dilemma

Whether you're contemplating buying a chaise longue at a flea market or a bookcase from some guy online, you very well might find yourself wracked with indecision. There's always a bit of a gamble involved when you spot something you like but aren't sure you should really buy. Maybe you're not certain you actually need that pristine pink fifties sectional, or maybe you suspect the price tag may indicate just a tad more money than you really want to spend. Yes, rash spending can be a bad, bad thing for your wallet. And if an item sits around without a buyer for long enough, the seller will generally be willing to let you haggle down the price a bit more. But waiting that extra week, or day, or even minute could well mean that some other, more decisive secondhand shopper will have already snatched up your prize—and you'll be left wishing you'd taken your chance when you had it (hindsight truly is a curse).

My basic philosophy is this: If you love it, want it, need it, can't bear not to have it, then don't bother to wait till day two on the off chance that you may get an even better deal. Heck, don't even wait an extra fifteen minutes to debate whether you should take the risk, because your indecision could cost you that beloved chair/coffee table/weird, abstractly zoomorphic vintage lamp. If, on the other hand, life will roll along just merrily without you carting that goodie home, then go ahead, take the gamble: Should you lose out this time, it's just another good excuse to keep on shopping.

space out

Your hand-me-down sofa, those revamped thrift-store end tables, that coffee table you rescued from down the block on trash day, your brand-new IKEA bookcases—there they sit, pushed aside into a corner, just waiting for you to find that perfect place for each and every one in your digs. So many objects, so many possibilities. . . .

And there you are, without a clue what to do next.

It's perfectly understandable. After all, there's something kind of intimidating about the sight of that empty expanse of a room and that lineup of furnishings, all waiting expectantly for you to make some sort of decision about their fate. Your first inclination might be to find some spare wall space and slide in whatever item will fit, but when this strategy leaves you with a sofa that's so far away from the television that you'd need binoculars to make out the action on screen, you realize it's time to find a better method for arranging your goods. Still, before you start dragging and shoving those heavy pieces of furniture from corner to corner, wall to wall, hoping to magically stumble upon the optimal configuration, hold on there, cowboy, and take the time to think before you act.

Sit down, get comfy, and make some plans. As anal-retentive as this might seem, it's actually the lazy way out. You'll be saving yourself a lot of unnecessary sweat and potential stubbed toes by waiting until you've performed a solid analysis of the situation. Take a long, hard look at your room and your stuff, and put the old noggin to work. Now's the time to think about what you want to do in your room, what you want your room to do for you, and how your furniture can help you accomplish it all.

plan it out on paper

No matter how fertile an imagination you might possess, it's hard to get a good sense of whether this big bulky sofa is going to fit into that bitty corner of the room by just picturing the scene in your brain. Here's where a little arts-and-crafts fun comes to the rescue.

Get yourself some graph paper and a writing implement. Grab a tape measure and measure the dimensions of your room, then make a scale drawing of the space on your graph paper. A convenient scale for a normal-sized room might be ½" on paper equals 1' actual space. Once you have your room dimensions down, measure the positions of any fixtures that you'll have to work around when arranging furniture—windows, fireplaces, radiators, doorways. Draw these fixtures onto that floor plan sketch, labeling each object so you'll remember what's what. Make sure you leave enough room for any door that has to open; sketch in an arc to indicate its swing.

Next, measure every major piece of furniture that you're planning to put in the room, from sofas and bookcases to floor lamps and end tables. Using the same scale that you've chosen for your floor plan, cut out an appropriately sized "footprint" for each of your furnishings. You can use colored construction paper if you're feeling fancy and assign different colors to represent different types of furnishing. Or just use regular old paper, shaded in with pen or marker to help the shape stand out against the graph paper floor plan. Again, make sure that you label each object.

With your customized playing board (a.k.a. floor plan) and playing pieces (a.k.a. furniture cutouts) set out in front of you, you're ready to start playing the furniture arrangement game—no heavy lifting required.

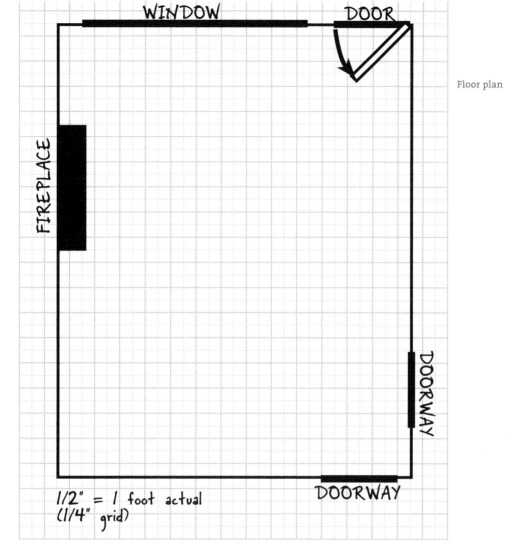

WINDOW

DOOR

Floor plan

FIREPLACE

DOORWAY

1/2" = 1 foot actual
(1/4" grid)

DOORWAY

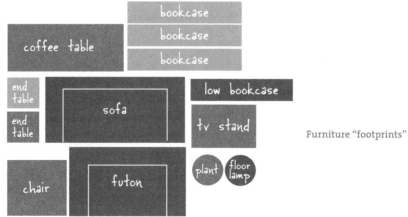

bookcase

bookcase

bookcase

coffee table

end table

end table

low bookcase

sofa

tv stand

chair

futon

plant

floor lamp

Furniture "footprints"

a room with a view

One of the big questions you should ask yourself when you're figuring out what to put exactly where: What do you want to be looking at when you're sitting in this room? This is what the pros are babbling about when they talk about "finding the focal point." Many rooms have a logical focal point. In your living room, for instance, it could be a big window with a nice view outside, or, if you're really lucky, a fireplace. In the bedroom, it could be another window, or even a vast expanse of wall where your favorite artwork could be proudly displayed. Once you have a sense of what your ideal vantage point might be in a given room, you'll know in which direction you should try to orient your major furnishings. Don't panic if a long perusal and numerous laps around the room reveal nothing particularly interesting to look at, no matter where you stand. Think of it as an opportunity: If you're working with a big, bland box without any built-in details of note, you have a nice blank canvas to work with. Choose a favorite furnishing, pick a prime spot for it, and work from there.

start big

Once you've thought about how to place your furnishings, you're ready to begin playing around with potential locations for your goods. Start with the big stuff. In the living room, that'll probably mean the entertainment center/TV cart and the sofa; in the bedroom, your bed; in the office, your desk. The logic to this is simple: The bigger the piece of furniture, the fewer potential places that can physically accommodate that piece. Moreover, once you have your major items sensibly situated, the smaller furnishings will mostly fall right into place. Placing the sofa, for instance, tells you exactly where the coffee table should go so you have a handy spot to keep the remote control and kick up your feet. Positioning the bed tells you where your nightstands ought to go if you want a place to stack your bedtime reading. Finding a prime spot for your desk helps you see where you should plop that floor lamp so you don't have to strain your eyes while you kill time online—*err*, telecommute. So think big when you're starting the arrangement process—find the perfect place for each of the major items first, and fuss with your beloved snapshots and tchotchkes later.

A brief word of advice regarding the old boob tube: Unless you're a member of that tiny subset of modern Americans who've made a conscious decision to shun the evils of TV, your living room—at least—will feature a television set. And unless you actually like the tangled A/V cable aesthetic, that television will be pushed up against one of the walls. If it all possible, don't place your TV directly opposite a window—you'll pretty much guarantee that you'll never watch it during the daytime, as the glare will drive you bonkers. Having said that, let me admit now that in my last nest, my TV was, in fact, situated directly opposite a gargantuan window. Ninety-nine percent of the time this was just fine, as soap operas and football games and other daytime fare are not high on my must-see TV list anyway. But every once in a while, I'd seized by the urge to spend a lazy Sunday afternoon camped out on the sofa with my Buffy DVDs. It's a testament to my Buffy addiction that I still managed to persist despite the fact that I could barely see the picture on the screen. If you plan on doing any significant amount of television viewing during daylight hours, do yourself a favor from the get-go, and find a sensible spot for the set where window glare won't be a problem.

go with the flow

There are certain areas of each room where you won't be able to place any furniture because doing so would make it pretty damn awkward to navigate around the room. So one of the major factors you'll want to keep in mind as you're shuffling your little furniture pieces about is the room's flow.

The ability to get from one point to another without banging into an obstacle is basically what interior designers mean by flow. Doorways largely dictate flow. Because we humans tend to be a lazy lot, we generally like to be able to get from one doorway to another doorway in as straight a line as possible, to avoid having to walk any longer than absolutely necessary. Which means that you generally won't want to plop a gargantuan sofa smack dab in the middle of that line of flow between two entryways. Yes, you *can* have a piece of furniture partially jutting into that traffic path—and in the cramped quarters of the sort your typical postcollege entry-level income permits, there might be no avoiding it—but you just don't want to obstruct that path completely. Keep in mind that two and a half feet is pretty much the minimum you can get away with when it comes to a comfortable path width. Also bear in mind that certain items of furniture will affect how you want to direct the traffic flow. It's a bad idea, for instance, to arrange your sofa and chairs in such a way that it is physically impossible to get across the room without cutting right in front of the sofa, as this can make it mighty annoying when folks are trying to have a chat.

the finer points

Choose your focal points, place the big objects first, and pay attention to a room's natural traffic flow, and your first pad will probably already look a thousand times better than your old dorm room ever did. But if you've done all that and still feel like there's just something not quite right about how your stuff sits in your space, here are a few more tricks for better furniture arranging.

Don't neglect function. Functionality is as important as aesthetics when it comes to good furniture arrangement. Think about what you want to be doing while you're in your living room, kitchen, spare room, bedroom (get your mind out of the gutter!) and arrange the furniture accordingly. For example, sofas and chairs should be a comfortable distance away from the TV. If you've got a tiny little TV, scoot those couches up close; if you're the proud owner of a huge monstrosity of a boob tube, set the seating farther back. In the bedroom, pay attention to where you sit the bed in relation to the window. If you need morning sun smacking you sidelong in the face to wake up in the morning, slide your bed up close to the window. If there's a neon sign blaring opposite your window, tuck the bed in a corner where that glaring light won't be streaming in your face as you try to get to sleep each night.

Get a little closer. When setting up their living rooms, one of the biggest mistakes people make is to place the seating too far apart. Think about conversational distances when you're planning. If you're sitting on sofa A, where do you want your guests to be sitting to make conversation feel natural? In general, it doesn't work to place two sofas on opposite walls, facing each other square on, because that's a strange setup for conversing—it kind of makes you feel like you're in a doctor's waiting room or sitting on a subway, right? Placing the sofas at an angle to one another feels far more comfortable and homey.

Step away from the wall. Most people think that the best place to put the furniture is flat up against the walls—that way you get maximum open floor space, right? Well, kind of, but sometimes all that open floor space isn't a good thing. It's true that if you've got big furniture in teeny-tiny spaces, you'll often have no choice but to place your furniture against those walls. In larger spaces, however, that's often the least inviting arrangement possible. By placing everything against the wall, you're left with this strange empty space in the middle of the room that makes all the stuff on the edges feel isolated. Some items probably have to go against the walls—entertainment centers, ceiling-high bookcases and the like tend to look mighty odd floating in the middle of a room (although a set of shorter bookcases or open bookcases can be used effectively in a large, long room as a room divider). But lower pieces, like sofas, armchairs, and tables, often look better when there's some space behind them. Besides, you'll suddenly find that you have a whole lot more space to work with when you're not restricting yourself to the perimeter of the room. So don't be afraid to pull that sofa out and away

an awkward arrangement . . .

Your first instinct may be to push everything against the wall to get maximum open floor space. But unless you live in a closet, this often results in a room that feels awkward and uninviting. Your room might look spacious, true, but you also end up having to run an obstacle course to cross from one door to the next because there's a great big love seat and coffee table plopped in the middle of your path; you find you have to stop renting movies with subtitles because you can't read the text on the screen from your perch all the way on the other side of the room. And when you still can't find room for that much-needed additional bookcase, you'll likely find that your formerly open, airy space soon becomes cluttered with piles of homeless books and CDs and DVDs.

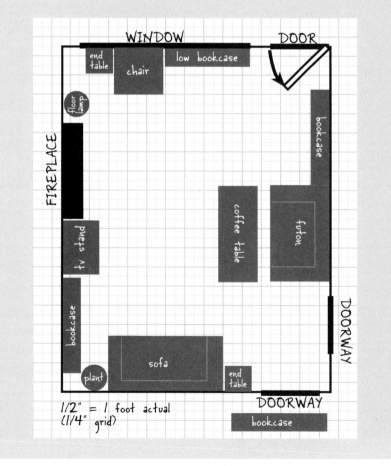

a better way . . .

Sliding some shorter pieces—like sofas and tables—away from the edges of the room and positioning a few items on the diagonal can create a much cozier sense of space, letting you use your space as efficiently as possible. You might have less floor space in general than if you were to stick with the flat-against-the-wall method of room nondesign, but what you'll find is that every bit of the room now feels usable. Instead of a big black hole in the center, you have a comfortable hangout and TV viewing area around the fireplace, plus a separate reading nook for when you need some quiet time. Moreover, you can easily get from one doorway to another without smacking into a big piece of furniture or rudely cutting in front of other folks when they're deep in conversation or glued to the TV screen.

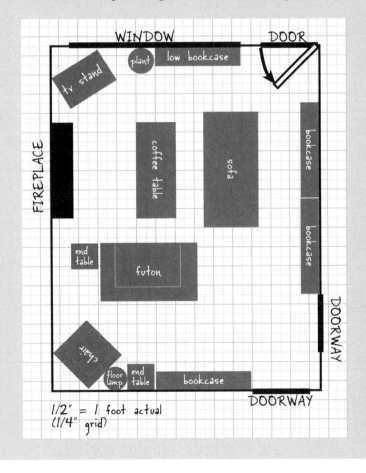

from the wall. Even if you only have enough room to pull it out 8" or so, you may find that you now have a good spot to place that funky floor lamp, or one of those narrow sofa tables.

Try a different angle. Once you've moved away from the wall, open yourself to another wacky thought: Furniture can go at an angle that's not parallel to any single wall! Placing a piece of furniture at an angle other than parallel or perpendicular to the walls often helps to soften the geometry of the room—you end up with a room that feels less boxy and formal, more relaxed and fun.

Multitask it. Unless you're lucky enough to have scored a mansion as your first digs, you're probably working with a limited amount of living space. To get the maximum amount of living out of that space, it's a good idea to multitask your rooms whenever possible. Is there a way to divide up the big living room so you can fit in a dining area on one end and a hangout space on the other? Can you move that futon sofa from the living room to the little second bedroom and turn it into an office cum guest room? Can you slide a small desk into that big closet and use it for a makeshift office as well as storage? Get your rooms to serve double duty and you'll find that even the smallest of apartments can give you plenty of space for all your living needs.

décor dilemmas: cluttered place versus spartan space

Every apartment and every house comes with its own set of distinctly personal quirks. My own home, for instance, has the vexing characteristic of having just about everything that's preinstalled—lighting fixtures, bathroom vanity, medicine cabinets, you name it—aligned to absolutely nothing, and, if it comes as part of a pair, just slightly askew from its mate. Certain decorating problems, however, seem universal to the quasi-adult living experience. Whether it's because what little cash we have goes toward student loans, food, and rent, or we're just too swamped with work and play, the end result is that our abodes have a natural tendency toward one of two extremes—the cluttered, "I can't resist buying every piece of junk I find at the flea market" place, or the spartan, "I'm too lazy to decorate" space. You know which category you fall under. Either way, here's help. Here's how to make more space when you're convinced you don't have anywhere near enough, and advice on how to fill the void when you're not gifted in the accumulating arts.

the cluttered place

The symptoms. You know you're nursing a serious cramped pad problem if you've got:

* Stacks of books, CDs, and videotapes piled up in precarious towers on top of that one crammed little bookcase, spilling over onto the floor, the coffee table, the kitchen table, and so on.

* A hodgepodge of sofas and chairs, in clashing colors and patterns, squeezed so tightly into your living room that there's barely room to walk.

* No wall visible because it's packed end-to-end, floor-to-ceiling with extra chairs and little end tables, posters and snapshots and post- cards, your candy wrapper collection, that placemat from the Chinese restaurant where you and your sweetie went on your first date—in short, stuff, stuff, and more stuff.

The remedy

Reconsider the necessities. Take a good look at the furnishings and pare the room's stock down to the essentials. Spare chairs can be moved to other rooms, bookcases can be moved to narrow hallways and entry- ways that don't get much other use, and a dresser can sometimes be squeezed into the closet.

Sky's the limit! Remember the ceiling. There's no reason that every single item of furnishing has to sit directly on the floor. Do a little rearranging and you might find that you can place short bookcases and file cabinets on top of one another to take up less floor space (although you'll want to make certain it's stable), or stack extra dining chairs and store them in a corner when they aren't in use.

Change your focus. Don't position your main seating area so it's staring directly at a big messy wall of mismatched bookshelves or those towers of storage containers. Hide the bookcases behind the main seating area; slide the boxes underneath the end tables. Yes, you have a lot of stuff, but find an inconspicuous spot for the junk.

Control your color. Paint your walls, bookcases, and cabinets in a single color and you'll instantly make your small space feel more open. Got five different types of wood grain represented in your furniture offerings? Cover it all up with paint and you've got an instant matching set. White gives you a nice clean canvas, and gives the illusion of more space, but it's certainly not the only option. What's most important is that you keep the number of different, competing shades to a minimum. Sticking with solids and avoiding patterns will also help to minimize the visual chaos and make the space seem more expansive.

the spartan space

The symptoms. You know your space is uninvitingly spartan if:

* The sum total of your room's inventory consists of less than three items of furnishing.

* You're using cardboard boxes as a TV stand, bedside table, and sofa end table—basically, for any function other than storage or shipping.

* You find your eye lingering over every stain, crack, and nail hole in the vast, stark, naked expanse of your walls.

* Sound echoes, bouncing unimpeded off the bare walls, as there's simply no stuff in between to absorb or block it.

✴ Visitors ask you how you're liking your new place when you've already been living there for a year and a half.

The remedy

Bring it together. Most folks like to maximize their space, but big really isn't always a good thing. That vast empty space in the middle of your spartan space, for example—that might as well have a great big sign claiming no man's land. And having an isolated chair on one side of the room and a sofa all the way on the other just makes your "arrangement" look random. Move your stuff away from the walls and bring everything a little closer together—you'll find it feels a whole lot cozier when you can actually talk to a friend sitting in the other chair without having to project your voice all the way across the room.

Get diagonal. Consider rotating big items so they're at an angle. They'll jut out more and sit more assertively in the space.

Do a balancing act. Make sure you don't have all your big items and major focal points on one side of the room. If your living room has a big fireplace, for example, try sliding that entertainment center to the opposite side of the room to balance it out. If for some reason you like your furniture all pushed up against one end of the room, throw a great big painting up on the other end or paint it a fun loud color.

Invest in an area rug. So, what little furniture you have just floats in that big empty floor space, does it? Lucky you. Space is indeed a luxury, but to help create a cozier ambience—even if all you've got is a TV and a sofa—define the sitting area with a rug.

Whether you're dealing with too much space or too few goods to fill it, a good rearrangement is often the quickest way to pep up a blah pad. Best of all, it costs you absolutely *nada,* beyond an hour or two of your free time. Which is why this is one apartment makeover project that even the most fiscally challenged among us can easily swing.

chapter five

lighten up

ask any artist and they'll tell you this: Never underestimate the importance of lighting. The right lighting can make a big space look soothingly airy rather than coldly cavernous, and a small space comfortably snug rather than just plain cramped; it can transform a completely ordinary place into a moodily evocative space. Poor lighting, on the other hand, renders the most carefully decorated room flatly uninviting. That bland, plastic-domed ceiling fixture that came with your new digs is a prime example of bad lighting. Yes, it serves the basic function of allowing you to make out what's in the room long after the sun goes down. But if the fixture is new it's probably too bright to give your room any semblance of ambience, and if it's old, it's likely to be so dim that you find your eyes straining to see even when it's on. The good news, for those of us for whom money is indeed a great big fat object, is that fab lighting can be achieved pretty easily even without a hefty cash investment. The right placement, and a solid sense of the disadvantages and advantages of the various types of lighting available, can make all the difference in the world.

Nothing beats the light you get from honest-to-goodness, all-natural sunshine: It's bright; it's a happy, lovely, pure-white color; and best of all, using it doesn't increase your electric bill. So the first step in lighting your abode is making sure you take maximum advantage of the natural stuff.

While some abodes will always be sunnier than others, based on how big and numerous the windows are and which direction they happen to be facing, there are still a few small changes that even renters can make to brighten things up. Ditch the heavy drapery and swap or layer in some breezier sheers; these translucent fabrics will let in more light from your windows on sunny days. Heck, if privacy isn't a big issue, go completely bare. Additionally, you can hang a big mirror opposite your window to amplify the sunlight. And yes, though housekeeping is a bore, it really will help a lot if you remember to give those windows a clean from time to time.

Natural light alone, however, is rarely sufficient. Even if that whole sunset phenomenon were an issue, you'd probably find that there are times of day and areas of your apartment where a little extra lighting help is in order. When the sun doesn't provide us with the light we need, it's time to fake it.

Artificial lighting basically falls into three main categories:

1. General ambient lighting (moderately bright, diffuse, covers a large area)

2. Task/spot lighting (very bright, focused, direct, covers a small area)

3. Mood lighting (soft, dim, diffuse, covers a small area)

Most rooms will require a combination of these three types of lighting to allow you the flexibility to adjust your lighting levels to suit the many activities that might take place within each. In my first postcollege apartment, the living room was the dining room, the reading room, the entertaining room, the project room, and the guest room, all wrapped up into one small space. I rapidly learned that different situations called for very different lighting, and that no single light source was going to meet every single one of my needs. If many of the rooms in your pad serve multiple functions, as is so often the case in our very humble first abodes, you will find it's especially important that your room has enough different lighting options to take you from morning to evening, weekday to weekend.

When you're trying to clean, for example, you'll want as much general overhead lighting as possible so you can make sure you hit every nook and cranny with that dust cloth—or at least vacuum up those monster dust bunnies that have a tendency to breed in the corners. When you're reading a book, you'll need bright, focused light to illuminate your pages. And if you're throwing a romantic dinner for two, you'll want soft, flattering lighting that helps you and your date look your most irresistible, and creates an appropriately sexy atmosphere for any postmeal activities. Basically, unless you're dealing with a tiny room that serves one dedicated purpose, you'll find that a single light source just does not cut it.

If your knowledge of lighting begins and ends with that standard-issue dorm room staple, the halogen floor lamp, it's time to learn more about the many different kinds of lighting options that are available out there, and what each type can do for you.

general ambient lighting

You know the ceiling light that came preinstalled in your apartment, the one whose uniform but utterly unremarkable light seems somehow both too low for reading and too glaring for parties? That would fall into the general ambient category. Recessed track lighting, fluorescent ceiling lighting, wall sconces, and the aforementioned halogen floor lamps are other examples of general ambient lighting. The advantages of this sort of lighting are simple. To begin with, a few sources of general ambient lighting usually come built in to the apartment, which means you'll probably have them whether you like it or not. But more importantly, these sources can cast a moderately bright level of light over a large area, which means you get a fair amount of coverage for your buck.

Adding more sources of general ambient lighting can brighten an entire room, making small rooms appear larger and dark-colored spaces feel warmer and more inviting. They also even out the lighting in a room when you're watching television or playing video games, which is a good thing, considering that the glare of the screen in contrast to pitch black surround-

Ambient lighting

ings can tax your eyes and inflict some nasty headaches. Because general ambient light sources illuminate over a large space, however, they give you very little control over any areas in a room that you might especially like to highlight—a series of framed photos from your backpacking adventures across Europe, a painting your art-major college roomie gave you, your sleek new glass-front bookcase, the antique curved-leg table you inherited from your grandmother. They also never seem to provide quite enough light when you're trying to perform tasks such as reading a book, scribbling in your journal, poring over a stack of bills, or working on your latest crafty project.

task/spot lighting

Task/spot lamps provide very bright, very focused light that can be used to illuminate specific areas of interest in a room. A task/spot light is generally a lamp whose bulb is semienclosed in a reflective casing, and whose head can be aimed in various directions. Desk lamps and spotlights belong in this category, as well as floor lamps and track lamps that have adjustable heads.

When evaluating your lighting needs, think about where you sit in the room when you're doing those tasks that require good lighting. If you've got a favorite comfy armchair where you like to curl up and read, it makes sense to place a lamp with an adjustable head nearby, so that you can aim the light to fall directly over your pages whenever you play bookworm. Your worktable, too, will require either a good desk lamp (lamps with halogen bulbs are great, since they provide an intense white light) or a bright hanging lamp (you'll want something that reflects the light down, rather than a hanging lamp that encloses the bulb in a translucent shell). Basically, any room in which you'll be spending large amounts of time trying to actually do stuff—whether that's work, pleasure reading, or your DIY project of the moment—will require some sort of task/spot lighting.

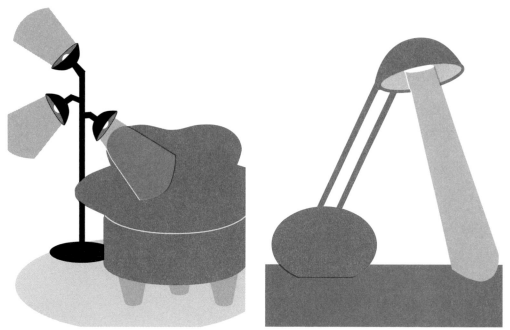

Task lighting

mood lighting

We generally think of lighting as serving a highly practical function. Both general ambient and task/spot lighting are essentially utilitarian in purpose: They make it easier to see what you're doing. But lighting can also be used decoratively—to create a specific mood, to add a sense of character to a space. And as anyone who's ever been to a romantic restaurant or a swanky bar will attest, soft, dim lighting is infinitely more relaxing than bright lighting. So while it's not totally practical, mood lighting is nonetheless essential in any room that's going to be used for throwing parties and engaging in other fun pursuits—in other words, pretty much every room except the office.

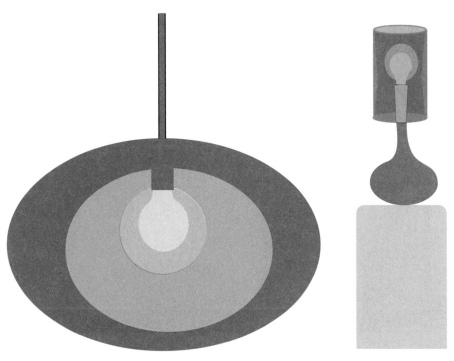

Mood lighting

Placing a smattering of nicely shaped small table lamps strategically around the room is an easy way to define conversational areas, those little nooks that are perfect for intimate chats. In the bedroom and the living room, especially, they're a must. In hallways and foyers, where all you really want is enough light to avoid bumping into the walls, some good mood lighting might be all the illumination you need. Try a hanging lamp with a beautiful translucent shade and a low-wattage, warm-toned bulb—Japanese-style paper globes, available through IKEA and other budget furniture stores, are unbelievably cheap and look sleek and modern. Diffuse hanging lamps are also a great way to softly light up the dark corners of rooms, giving small spaces the illusion of being more expansive than they actually are.

Play around with colored lights as well—blue feels a bit funky, red fun and festive, and the ever-popular, kitschy-cool black lighting (ultraviolet) always seems to be a big hit with guests. Task/spot lighting can also be transformed to suit your mood-lighting needs. Just replace the regular bulb with a low-wattage bulb, then aim the lamp at a wall or ceiling; the reflected light will cast a lovely, soft glow. Alternatively, co-opt those little Christmas lights you used to pull out only at holiday times; string them along the walls by the ceiling, lace them through houseplants, or coil up the whole string and arrange in a glass vase. Last but not least, every pad should include a few candles. In addition to coming in mighty handy during the occasional blackout, you just can't beat candlelight for adding some serious sexy to your space.

bulb basics

While the shape and positioning of your lighting sources will play a big role in how they serve to illuminate your abode, the type of bulb you pop into each lamp will also have a major impact. As a trip to any hardware store will reveal, lightbulbs come in many varieties. Here's a brief explanation of the three main types you're likely to encounter.

Incandescent. These are the ones that you probably picture when you think of lightbulbs, the kinds that screw into their sockets. Incandescent bulbs are cheap, which is a big part of the reason they're so ubiquitous. The downside is that they're pretty energy-inefficient, giving off a fair amount of heat—and this means higher electricity bills and bulbs that need to be replaced frequently. Still, they give off a warm, rosy-golden tone that instantly cozies up any room. If you do decide to go with an incandescent, keep in mind that pearl bulbs offer a softer light, but clear bulbs a brighter one.

Fluorescent. For a long time, I ignored fluorescent bulbs altogether because I associated them with those awful tube lights, the ones that pop into a translucent panel in the ceiling, the kind you probably have in your office at work. Those fluorescents generally give off a cool, bluish-green tone that's universally unflattering to skin tones. Fortunately, advances in lightbulb technology have brought us much more pleasant warm-toned fluorescents. Most importantly, you can now find so-called compact fluorescents that can make a smart alternative to the incandescent bulb. Aesthetics-wise, I still prefer the richer tone of incandescent bulbs, and per bulb, compact fluorescents are much pricier. However, the upside of fluorescents is that they don't give off much heat and beat the pants off incandescents in the energy efficiency department. For this reason, you might want to consider using compact fluorescent bulbs in place of incandescents, especially in lamps that stay on for long periods at a time. They're good for your electric bills as well as for the general well-being of the planet. Do make sure to look for bulbs that are explicitly labeled "warm white," unless you actually like the way traditional fluorescent bulbs make your skin look sickly.

Halogen. Generally, lamps designed for halogen bulbs will accept only this type of bulb. Halogen bulbs give off an intense, pure white light that makes them ideal for task lighting. When changing halogen bulbs, be sure not to let the oils on your grubby little digits get all over the bulb, as this shortens the bulb's lifespan.

furnishings first aid: how to repair a lamp

There it sat, amid a legion of other abandoned housewares, collecting dust next to a record player relic: our soon-to-be latest lamp acquisition. It was little, it was brown, it had a sketchy-looking old black cord, and it had probably been sitting on that grimy shelf at the back of Value Village for weeks before my boyfriend and I stumbled upon it. Neither of us could quite figure out exactly how it was meant to be used—it wasn't obviously a floor lamp, or a table lamp, or a hanging lamp, just a small spherical metal lamp shade with a long cord attached. But scrawled across its murky-brown curves, in red grease pencil, was the irresistible price of one dollar. We happily snatched it up, carried it off to the cash register, plunked down a buck, and brought it back home. Sure it was in need of a little first aid, but so what? It was a bargain, and so funky . . . or rather it would be, once we made a few minor modifications.

There's something a little scary about buying an electrical appliance secondhand. There's just no way of knowing, until you've taken the risk and carried it back to your apartment, whether the thing actually functions or not. And since thrift shops, flea markets, yard sales, and the like offer no warranty whatsoever, you're out of luck if the answer should be the latter, right? When you're dealing with lamps, the answer is an emphatic no sir-ree. Cloth shades can be replaced, metal shades spray painted. And if your lamp yields no light when you plug in the cord, the solution is generally as simple as either replacing the entire socket or even just the cord.

Here's a step-by-step guide to repairing that broken lamp. Every lamp is assembled a little bit differently, but once you've seen one lamp's innards—and learned the super-easy steps for disassembling/reassembling the parts—you'll pretty much be equipped to handle any incandescent lamp.

The toolkit:

* Screwdriver

* Extension cord

* Wire strippers (or at least a Swiss Army knife, should you lack the former)

* Tin snips (or scissors that you don't mind potentially dulling, Swiss Army knife, razor knife . . . in other words, something sharp that can cut through the extension cord)

The directions:

1. The first step is to make certain that the issue isn't just a bad bulb. Test your original bulb in a lamp that you know works. If the bulb's fine, proceed to Step 2.

2. Unplug your lamp. Yes, physically disconnect the cord from the outlet; just turning your lamp off isn't going to cut it, safety-wise. Inspect the plug; if the prongs look worn or the casing's cracked, try replacing the plug. You can buy replacement plugs at any home improvement or hardware store; follow the directions that come with your specific plug to attach it to the cord.

3. If the bulb and plug look fine, take a look at the cord. Is it frayed? Does wiggling it around into just the right position get the light to go on? If so, you might just need a new cord. On the other hand, if the cord looks okay, it's likely that you need a new socket. Either way, it's time to get more invasive with your lamp surgery.

4. Remove the bulb and the lampshade and set them aside. (If you're looking to pep up the shade, you can either mosey over to any store that sells lamps and buy yourself a brand-new lampshade replacement, get a new-to-you shade at your local thrift shop, or revamp your existing shade.)

5. Now you'll need access to the socket, and in particular its interior, where the wires of the cord connect to the terminals. Your standard socket will have an outer sleeve at the top that's marked with the word "press." Squeeze there. If it's particularly stubborn, use pliers or

press with a screwdriver. Remove the sleeve, and you should now find yourself faced with the inside of the socket.

6. If this peek inside reveals that the wires have just come detached, your repair job's as simple as loosening the terminal screws, reattaching the wires, and putting the whole thing back together. Otherwise, use a screwdriver to loosen the screws, and detach the wires from the socket.

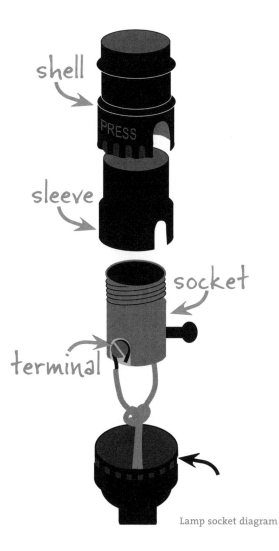

Lamp socket diagram

7. If all previous tests have revealed nothing obviously wrong with your lamp, your socket probably needs to be replaced. Take the old socket down to your hardware store, and look for a new socket that's the same style. If you've got a hardware-store phobia and can't make any sense of the lighting aisle, ask a friendly sales clerk where you can find a replacement for that socket you've got in your hand.

8. Even if the cord isn't obviously damaged, I generally replace it when I'm repairing an old lamp. This is where the extension cord comes in handy. Snip off the female end (that would be the nonplug end) of the extension cord and set it aside; it won't be used for this project. Carefully peel apart the two fused ends of the extension cord, separating them about 2" down the length of the cord. Using wire strippers, strip the two ends, exposing about ¾"–1" of wire. Alternatively, you can use a Swiss Army knife; hold the knife nearly, but not quite, parallel to the wire, and carefully slice through the plastic, away from you until you get to the wire. Do this all the way around the wire.

9. Snip off the plug end of the old cord and do the same thing you did in Step 6 to the new cord, splitting the cord and stripping about an inch. Twist each of the stripped wires from the new cord to the stripped wires from the old. Secure the connection with some tape. Now, pull the old cord gently from the socket cap end, using it to thread the new cord through the lamp base. When the new cord emerges, untape and detach the old cord, and discard it.

10. Your new cord should now be threaded through the lamp base, with the exposed ends coming out from the socket cap. At this point, the do-it-yourself guides will tell you to tie the two ends of the wire together into an underwriter's knot. It's supposed to reduce tension on the wires, presumably making it less likely for the wires to detach from the terminal. Confession time now: I'd rewired at least four lamps before learning about this knot, and so far, no

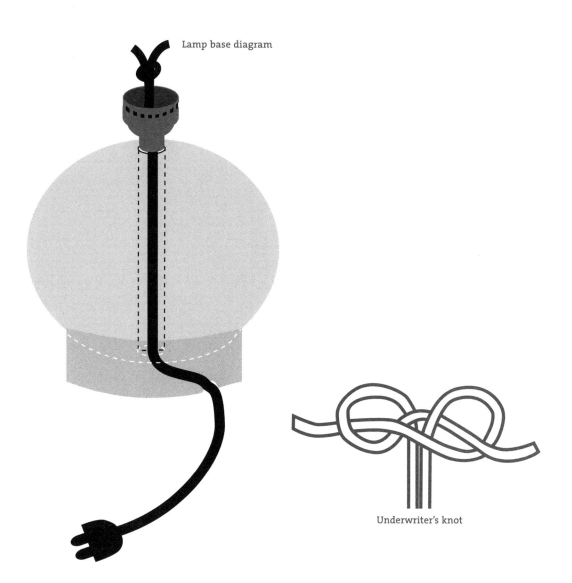

Lamp base diagram

Underwriter's knot

problems. Having said that, the proper technique is illustrated above, and you should probably follow it if there's sufficient room in your socket cap.

11. Bend each wire into a hook. Attach each hooked wire to one of the terminals on the socket; if your wires and socket are color-coded, as is generally the case, the neutral white wire (also distinguished by

its ridged covering) goes to the silver terminal, and the hot black wire to the brass. You'll want to make sure that you've got the hooks aiming off to the right, in such a way that when you tighten the screws (clockwise), the screw will be turning in the same direction that the hook is aiming.

12. Pull the wire taut so that the socket rests securely in the cap, then reassemble your lamp. Pop on your lampshade, screw in a bulb, and plug it in. Now let there be light!

quickie lighting improvements

So you've been seriously rethinking your décor and have come to a sad realization: Your lighting situation sucks. Before you go on a mad shopping spree to replace every lamp and lighting fixture in your apartment, here are a few inexpensive insta-fixes that can improve your existing lighting significantly.

Up the wattage. Check the maximum wattage on your lighting fixture or lamp. Go energy-efficient with a compact fluorescent and you can get a brighter bulb that gives you more light—without running the risk of shorting out the lamp.

Change the lampshade. In addition to pepping up your actual décor, changing the lampshade can have a noticeable impact on the quality of the light that you get from a given lamp. A translucent material will let out more light than something more opaque; a colored lampshade will generally mute the light more than a white one, and affect the tone of the light as well. You can find lampshades in just about every shape, size, and color your imagination could dream up; get them new at any store that sells lamps, or look for cheap secondhand offerings at your favorite neighborhood thrift store.

Get thee a lamp dimmer. Available at most DIY and hardware stores, this is essentially a short extension cord with a built-in dimmer switch.

Plug the dimmer cord into the wall socket and your lamp into the dimmer cord, and you can raise and lower your lighting to whatever level suits your mood. Note, however, that dimmers only work on incandescent bulbs, not fluorescent.

The right lighting can truly make or break a room. It defines the usability of a space and creates a sense of character. Best of all, it's one of the cheapest and simplest ways you can add style to your home, whether you're looking for lamps boasting funky shapes and interesting materials at garage sales, thrift shops, and budget furnishing purveyors, or giving the ho-hum lamps you already own a fun makeover. Design a room to accommodate a range of different lighting levels and you'll have a multifunctional space that will be as good for work as it will be for play.

post-posters

et me just say straight off the bat (and please, don't be offended): I hate posters. Yes, they're cheap; certainly, they can do a dandy job of covering a very large area of ugly apartment wall; and okay, some of them even feature lovely artwork. But there's something about those mass-produced prints created expressly for the purpose of decorating walls that reeks of corporate-manufactured, society-approved "good taste." Posters, by and large, have no character; they're about someone else's idea of what belongs on your walls. They might be fine for a doctor's office, the sort of sterile environment where the sole décor objective is simply not to affront. But in your own home, you can do better. The best walls I've seen all share one thing in common: They say something about the unique personality of the person who lives within their confines.

Back in the middle and high school days, decorating the walls of my bedroom meant plastering them from floor to ceiling with glossy magazine cutouts of cute celebrity heartthrobs and mammoth posters promoting my favorite bands. There was nothing like waking up to Bill-and-Ted-era Keanu's goofy smile or Bono earnestly singing for me alone. Maximum wall coverage was the goal, and the more stuff I could tack up to declare my loves and obsessions, the better. I used my walls to express me, and whether the outcome was attractive or not was completely irrelevant. But in college, I had an epiphany: Wall decorations could serve an aesthetic function! Up went the stereotypical college standards—Klimt's *Kiss,* Van Gogh's *Starry Night,* a whole slew of Matisse prints—and into the closet and trash went any hint of real personality. Clearly I'd moved to the other extreme—all looks and no substance, prefab-style that made my room look like every other college freshman girl's dorm room.

These days, I'd like to think I've finally learned to achieve the proper balance: creating walls that are both nice to look at and uniquely representative of *moi.* Admittedly, the fact that I was a visual arts major in college has helped—all those final projects from photo classes, drawing classes, printmaking classes, and the like have provided a generous supply of artwork from which to choose for display. I'm no Picasso or Cartier-Bresson, but there's something nice about the fact that the vast majority of what's on my walls are *my* creations—images with stories behind them, pictures that connect to my past, objects that provide a starting point for discussion with guests who come to visit.

a few ideas to get you started

Even if you've never taken an art class in your life, there are still plenty of ways to do something with your wall space that speaks distinctly about who you are.

black-and-white photos

For classic sophistication, you can't go wrong with a series of framed black-and-white photographs. If you ever took a basic photography class, sift through your old work prints and pull out your favorite images. Alternatively, start playing photographer now. Buy some black-and-white film or go digital, converting your images to gray scale in your photo-editing program of choice. Start snapping pictures of your friends, your family, your favorite scenic spots, your hometown, your beloved puppy, whatever;

once you've captured a few images you like, get them printed as large as you can afford (because yes, bigger is often better). Or if you're truly not adept with all things mechanical, ask Mom and Dad if they have any old black-and-white family photos they would be willing to pass along. Most of all, don't worry about whether your photos are good enough to merit display; instead, concentrate on finding images that actually mean something to you. Besides, you'll be surprised at what a nice white mat and a simple frame can do to transform your amateur shots into works of art.

retro magazine pictures

Spend some time sifting through your grandparents' basement or attic—pictures from old image-heavy magazines like *Life* and *National Geographic* can make for very cool wall art. The key here is to get a theme going so your pictures don't look like a random assortment of ancient magazine cutouts but a real collection. Start amassing food-themed pictures or vintage pinup ladies, fifties Americana shots or classic cowboy images—find some concept that interests you and start clipping. Vintage magazine art goes perfectly with furniture from the same period, but retro pictures are also a fun way to give any plain-Jane pad a sense of campy fun. Just make sure to pop your magazine clippings into mats and frames to avoid that junior-high locker collage look.

old record albums

While you're down in the basement rummaging through all the junk, chances are good that you'll run into a box of old vinyl as well. What to do with those scratched-up but once-beloved albums from days of yore? Frame or display them on a shelf, of course. Record albums frequently feature cover art with a style that is deeply, deeply emblematic of the times in which they were produced—making them a fun source for fifties, sixties, seventies, and eighties graphic design.

pressed flowers and leaves

Even if you don't have a single artistic bone in your body, you can create beautiful, one-of-a-kind artwork for your home by framing pressed flowers and other natural specimens. Go for a stroll on a sunny day and take the time to pick pretty wildflowers in lovely shades of yellow or purple, some nicely shaped leaves perhaps. When you get home, gently press them between two sheets of newsprint sandwiched in the pages of a big, heavy book—stack more books on top, check back on them in a week, and they should be thoroughly dried out and ready for framing.

Pressed plant art

funky thrift-shopped frames

Shop flea markets and secondhand shops for funky frames. They'll probably be housing a black velvet Elvis or cheesy waterfall, but try to ignore
that—what's important is that the frame style appeals to you. The ugly
"art" can go straight into the trash—though if it's so bad there's actually
something rather appealing about it, you can always go the kitsch route.
You could, of course, insert whatever other artwork you have on hand into
your new frame. But the frames themselves can also be the main feature.
Try turning the frame into a mirror; simply measure the dimensions, then
head off to a mirror retail store (you can find them under "mirrors" in the
Yellow Pages) to get a piece custom-cut to fit. Alternatively, don't put
anything in your frames at all. Paint your thrift shop finds in funky colors,
antique the finishes, or try your hand at decoupage; arrange them artfully
on your wall, and make the frames themselves the focus.

please do touch: tactile art

Don't get me wrong: I adore looking at art. I love touring galleries, roaming
museums, and browsing through big beautiful coffee table art books. But
there's one thing about the typical art experience that's always bugged
me: those foreboding all-cap PLEASE DO NOT TOUCH signs that have an
irksome tendency to dot the walls of institutions of fine art. Yes, I understand the terrible impact that thousands and thousands of grubby, germy,
oily little fingers might have upon a treasured work, but still, it's frustrating. If there's a canvas thick with layers of paint, a sculpture that sinuously
curves around in cool smooth stone, isn't it human nature to want to
touch? Sadly, those ever-vigilant guards are likely to escort you to the door
should you attempt to do so at a museum. But why not make a wall of tactile art for your home? Rummage through your cabinets, take a trip to the
hardware store, roam the aisles of a craft store or fabric store. Pick things
up and squeeze them, squash them, run your fingers over them (yeah, you
might get a few strange looks at the store, but trust me, it's fun). Bubble

wrap, self-expanding foam, corrugated cardboard, Astroturf, fake fur—if you can touch it without incurring injury, allergy, or death, and if you can cheaply and easily fit it into a frame, it's fair game for this wall art project. Frame a piece of each texture in identical frames—without the protective glass, of course—then throw them up on a big expanse of wall where you and your guests can enjoy hours of tactile enjoyment.

fabric wall art

So your landlord's strictly forbidden you to paint your walls, but you're dying to cover those dingy off-white walls with swathes of color or pattern? Try fabric wall art. No, I'm not talking about those unicorn tapestries that

the fine art of decoupage

"Decoupage" is just a fancy word for the age-old technique of cutting out images and pasting them onto something new. It's the sort of thing you probably did all the time in summer camp arts-and-crafts sessions, and the results can actually look pretty sophisticated. Just about any smooth surface works dandy for decoupaging—cardboard boxes, furniture, picture frames, you name it. You can find your images in magazines and art books, old calendars, wallpaper, wrapping paper, postcards, greeting cards, wherever. Don't want to wreck the original source? Need multiple copies of a single image? No worries; just scan and color–laser print, or make color photocopies. Once you have your images prepped, start arranging them on whatever surface you're decoupaging. When you're happy with the layout, glue down each image using a thin even layer of plain white glue; starting from the center of the image and working your out, press gently with a clean finger to get out all the wrinkles. Wipe up excess glue with a damp rag. Once all the images are adhered and have had sufficient time to dry, it's time to seal your masterpiece. You can brush on a solution of diluted white glue (three parts glue to one part water), but for better durability, buy a can of polyurethane varnish or clear acrylic spray. Whatever sealant you use, make sure to apply enough coats that the edges of the glued images feel nice and smooth.

Touchable art

your Aunt Milly favors in her summer cottage. Fabric wall hangings can be the epitome of hip, provided you score some cool fabrics, of course. Rummage around thrift stores or your parents' attic for vintage prints, spend some time at your local fabric store (remnant bins can offer some good bargains), co-opt some clearance-bin bedsheets, or eBay it. Once you have your fabric, decide how you want to display it. You can hem the edges, then slide in wooden dowels at the top and bottom to create a simple wall hanging, or pop your fabric into whatever picture frame suits your fancy. For a clean-edged, borderless look, you can also stretch fabric over a wooden frame the same way an artist might with a painting—get precut wooden stretcher bars at an art store, or buy some 1" × 1"s at a hardware store, cut them to the desired lengths, and assemble the frame using flat metal brackets and screws.

Modern art

diy modern art

On a visit to the Centre Pompidou in Paris, my brother, standing in front of an Yves Klein blue-painted block of canvas, had this revelation: "Hey, I could do that!" And yes, you can, too. Just buy a large piece of canvas at an art store, then paint it in a single solid color. It's an easy way to add bold swashes of color to any room of your house, without the commitment. Bored with the mango color? Repaint it lavender—or lemon, or kiwi, or plum, or ruby. You can buy prestretched canvas at any art store, or custom-stretch your own to get whatever dimensions suit your space. Arrange several different color blocks in a series for a look that feels *très* contemporary. And hey, who knows, after swooping your favorite hue across your first piece of canvas, you might even feel the call of some heretofore latent gift for painting. If so, indulge away.

go 3d: display your collectibles

Whether you're an obsessive accumulator of lunchboxes or Japanese snack packaging, sno globes or action figures, you can show off the years of work that went into building up your precious collection. Floating shelves (no ugly brackets showing) are a simultaneously chic and utilitarian way to make use of your bare wall space; you can snag them for quite cheap at budget furnishing shops, or browse online for directions for building your own. Open wall cubes are another sleek option for featuring your favorite goods. Essentially a thick-sided box mounted on the wall, the wall cube has an opening in the middle for you to display whatever treasure tickles your fancy. Install a few cubes and arrange them in a row or grid; add stuff. Voila—you've transformed your flat white wall into a pop art sculpture.

Remember that the term that "artwork" doesn't have to mean something drawn, photographed, or painted—anything you can mount in a frame, display on a shelf, or otherwise hang, adhere, or slather onto a vertical surface is fair game for dressing those wide, bare walls of a new apartment. So look beyond those posters that once adorned your dorm room walls. Let your walls speak for *you*.

matting matters

As a studio arts major at a college far better known for turning out future presidents, Pulitzer-prize winners, and Nobel laureates than famous artists, I endured a fair amount of flack for choosing a "fun" major that would leave me with so few "practical" skills. This, of course, was utter nonsense, since let's face it: Very little of what any of us actually learn in our liberal arts college courses is of direct relevance when it comes to real jobs. Besides, years later, I can't remember a speck of the organic chemistry I was forced to study back when I was still deluded enough to think I should

the pro's toolkit

* Mat cutter for cutting beveled edges

* Mat cutter for straight edges or exacto/utility knife

* Straightedge, preferably one made to go with the mat cutter in such a way that the mat cutter can hook onto the straightedge to help guide it along

* Yardstick with T-square on one end

* Extra mat board on which to make your cuts

* Pencil

But what if you're too cheap/lazy/minimalist to get the more specialized tools available for cutting mats? You can still cut your own mats; you just won't be able to get the pretty beveled windows.

a low-budget toolkit

* X-Acto/utility knife with sharp blade
* Yardstick with T-square on one end
* Extra cardboard on which to make your cuts
* Pencil

go to med school. But the things I learned in my art classes, like composing a picture, pairing colors, and taking note of how the objects in my environment relate to one another—these are the things that have stuck with me and have come in mighty handy as I put together my digs.

One of the most useful skills I learned back in my art student days was that you can pop just about any image into a mat, and it'll look ten times better on your wall than it would in its naked state. Furthermore, mats are essential if you're placing your pictures, especially photographs, into frames: They'll keep your pictures from eventually getting stuck to the glass. Trust me: It takes just one ruined treasured snapshot to ensure that you'll never again slide a beloved photo into a frame unmatted. Getting pictures professionally matted and framed is, however, a rather expensive endeavor. Fortunately, with a few choice tools, anyone with a little patience and a steady hand can cut mats that look every bit as good as you'd get at a frame shop.

getting equipped

If you're willing to invest in a specialized cutting tool, you'll be able to easily make professional-quality mats that have nice, beveled (angled) edges on the windows. Handheld mat cutters generally run about $20 or so and can be found at art and craft stores. If you want to get a little fancier, a mat cutting system consists of a straightedge with a hooked lip that holds the mat cutter in place while you're making your cuts. I have a Logan

Compact Mat Cutter that's served me very well in the five years or so that I've owned it—at around $80 to $100, it's not exactly cheap (although it's definitely one of the more affordable professional-type mat-cutting systems available—they can run upwards of $300). If you're planning on cutting mats often, as I do, it can be a worthwhile investment.

choosing a mat board

Go to any good art store and you'll find a plethora of mat boards to choose from, ranging in price from an affordable $5 or so to easily twice that. So what's the difference between the cheapo stuff and the more expensive versions? Why buy the pricier boards when the budget boards generally come in a wider range of color options?

The answer's simple: Cheap mat board isn't acid-free, and if you're concerned at all with protecting your artwork for years to come, you'll want to go with the museum-quality, archival versions. If, on the other hand, you're framing something that's not intended to stay in your permanent collection of wall art—that picture you cut out from last year's calendar, for instance—then low-end mat board will serve you just fine. And even non-acid-free mat board is much better for your artwork than cardboard. If budget is the only thing that's holding you back from buying the archival stuff, however, check to see if your art store has a discount section. Mat board is one of those things that easily gets dinged up by overly eager prospective customers, so you can frequently find slightly damaged board on sale.

how to mat

Matting requires a certain frame of mind: It's not a difficult job, but it can be tedious, and the surest way toward matting disaster is to attempt to do it when you're in a rush. Save your matting project for a lazy Sunday afternoon, when you're feeling properly Zenned out and have all the time in the world.

Materials

Mat board

Acid-free hinging tape, paper or linen (you should be able to find this at art and craft stores—paper is cheaper)

Acid-free photo mounting corners, or acid-free double-sided tape (use the former if you want to be able to remove your pictures from their mats and avoid getting adhesive all over the back of your precious artwork)

Mat cutter

Step by step. Measure your image to determine how big of a window you'll need for your mat. Note that the image size may or may not be the same as your paper size. If your picture extends all the way to the edges of the paper, allow an additional $\frac{1}{4}$" on all sides, to ensure that you won't be able to see how the photo is adhered through the window. If your picture is 8" × 10", for example, you'll need your window to be about 7.5" × 9.5".

Decide on approximately how thick of a border you'd like for a mat. I like to give my photos and artwork a pretty generous border (at least 2" for an 8" × 10" picture, thicker for bigger artwork). Matting a small work of art in an oversized frame can actually result in a pretty cool look; in general, I find it's better to err on the side of too big than too small when it comes to mat size.

Since getting frames made in custom sizes can get pretty pricey, it's a good idea to buy frames in standard sizes before starting to measure and cut your mats—bearing in mind the approximate border size you'd like for whatever you're framing, of course. For an 8" × 10" image, for instance, you'll probably want to get an 11" × 14" frame.

Once you have your frame in hand, take apart the frame. Measure the length and width of the glass (or frame backing) to figure out how big you'll need to cut your mat board. It's a good idea to get the exact measurements, since a frame that's labeled 11" × 14" is frequently actually a little smaller or a little bigger than that. Once you have your measurements, use a straightedge and X-Acto knife (or mat cutter with straight blade) to cut your board down to size. You'll need to cut two pieces of mat board to fit your frame.

If you're framing something that's not terribly important to you—something that you don't mind taping up on the back—you can do a quick-and-easy mat with just one piece of mat board. With the double board version, we'll be cutting a window in one of the pieces, and using the second one as a backing board to attach the picture in a way that will make it easily removable. The double board mat has the added benefit of looking nice enough to display even without a frame.

You should now have two pieces of mat board that slide perfectly into your frame. Set one piece aside for now. Place your image on the backside of the second piece of mat board to determine where to place your image. Centered smack dab in the middle is an obvious choice, but not the only aesthetically pleasing option—a small image in a large mat will sometimes look more balanced if you weight the bottom border by making it a tad taller than the top.

If you're math-phobic or just plain too lazy to bother with calculations, the easiest way to make sure the picture is centered is to place it approximately in the middle of the board. Measure the distance from the edge of the image to the edge of the mat board on both the left and right sides, then nudge the picture left or right as necessary until the two measurements are the same. Mark the placement for the left and right edges of the picture on the mat board using a light pencil mark. Use the same technique (if you can call it that) to determine the top-bottom placement.

At each mark, square your T-square with the edge of the mat board and line up the straightedge with the penciled mark. Extend each line well beyond where it meets another line at the corners.

If you're the precise sort who would rather work out the numbers instead of judging it by eye, subtract the image width from the frame width, then divide by two to determine the left-right border width. Subtract the image height from the frame height, then divide by two to determine the top-bottom border width.

Before you make any cuts, measure the penciled rectangle and make sure that it's no bigger than the size of your image (if anything, you should

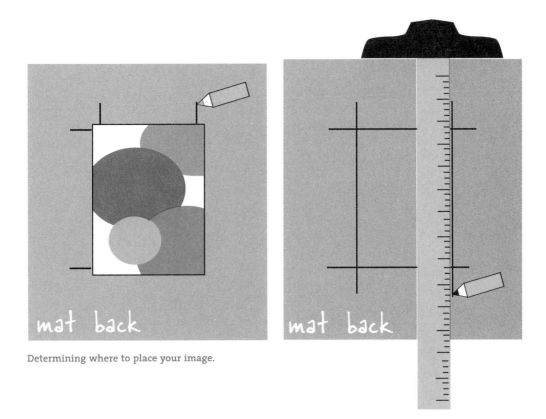

Determining where to place your image.

err on the very slightly smaller side, to make sure that your picture will completely fill the window once it's been cut). You'll also want to verify that the penciled rectangle sits square with respect to the edge of the mat board, using your T-square; you don't want to cut out the window only to realize that the window is actually kind of skewed.

Once you've made certain that you've measured everything properly, you're ready to cut out that window. If you're using a mat cutter, just follow the directions that come with your specific tool. If you're going low-tech, use that yardstick as a guide, and line it up with your pencil marks. Don't try and cut the board in a single go—score the mat board with your first cut to create a guide for the knife, then go over the same cut until you've sliced through the board. Be extra careful when you reach the corners.

Pop out the inner rectangle of mat board and save it for future projects.

Congratulations! You now have one piece of mat board with a lovely window cut out of the middle, along with a second piece of solid mat

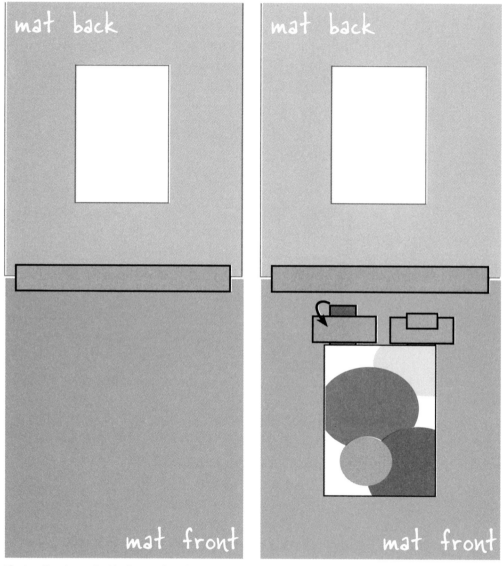

Placing the picture inside the mat board.

board. Place the window piece front-side down. Line up the top edge of the solid piece, front-side up, with the bottom edge of the window mat. Cut a piece of hinging tape that's about the same width as the mat, then moisten it with a damp sponge. Press the tape down so that half of it sticks to the bottom edge of the window mat and the other half sticks to the top of the solid mat. You should now have a lovely hinged mat.

With the mat open, place your picture so that it sits approximately in the center of the back piece of board. Close the window to check the picture position; partially lift the window and adjust the picture until it's aligned properly. Carefully lift up the window, making certain not to move the picture as you do so (you can weight the picture with something soft, smooth, and nondamaging if you're so inclined—wrap your weight in cloth if necessary—though I generally find it unnecessary to bother with the weight at all).

If you're using double-sided tape, just tape the picture down at the top two corners. If you're using photo corners on the other hand, proceed as follows: Lightly mark the corners of the picture using a pencil, and remove the picture. Stick photo corners on each corner of the picture, and line up the picture with the pencil marks you just drew. Close the window to make sure that nothing's shifted and the picture sits well in the window; open the window, then firmly press down the corners.

There's actually a third method you can use to attach your artwork to the mat board, using your acid-free hinging tape. With the image held in place (with this method, you'll definitely want to weight it), carefully attach two short strips of tape (about 3") at the top of the image, sticky-side up, and in such a way that half the tape adheres to the back of the image, while the other half extends above it. Cut two more short strips of tape and use them to hold the first two strips in place against the mat board; just press them down so that they sit parallel and just above the top edge of the artwork. Fold down the remaining exposed bits of vertical tape, and stick them to the horizontal strips.

Close the window again. You're now the proud owner of a beautifully matted picture that's ready to be popped into its frame.

hang-up help

So you've finally decided what to put up on those vast, blank walls of your nest. Terrific—all you'll need to do is bang a few nails into the wall, then plop your pictures into place, right? Alas, there's a bit more to the process than that, and the first step is to decide what to put where.

Don't, I repeat do not, just start hammering nails into your walls. You'll save yourself a lot of work—and the potential wrath of your landlord, who I can guarantee is not a fan of the Swiss cheese look—if you do a little planning in advance. Sketches are the easiest way to experiment with different potential positions to place your wall art. Use graph paper and you can easily sketch to scale. Alternatively, cut out pieces of newsprint that are the size of your frames, then tack them on the wall with poster gum to get a sense of what works and what doesn't. Having an extra set of arms also comes in handy. It's next to impossible to judge what your pictures are going to look like and whether they're hanging level when you're standing there with your cheek pressed to the wall, holding the frames up for placement. Enlist the help of a patient friend and get him or her to hold up the frames while you stand back and ponder.

Still, if you're just now graduating from the slap-up-as-many-posters-as-possible school of wall decoration, how do you know whether your new makeshift masterpieces should go by the couch or the front door, above the kitchen table or your bed? Yes, poorly placed artwork can look worse than no artwork at all. So here are a few words of advice on arranging basics, guaranteed to get you accessorizing those walls like a pro in no time.

Use your pictures to bring emphasis to specific areas of the room. Take a good look at your room. Where do your eyes naturally wander when you first walk into the room? When you're sitting in your favorite sofa? When you're sitting where your guests usually sit? When you're leaving the room? These are the areas upon which you'll generally want to focus when deciding where to place your pictures. If these prime spots lack anything of interest to look at, then it's time to add

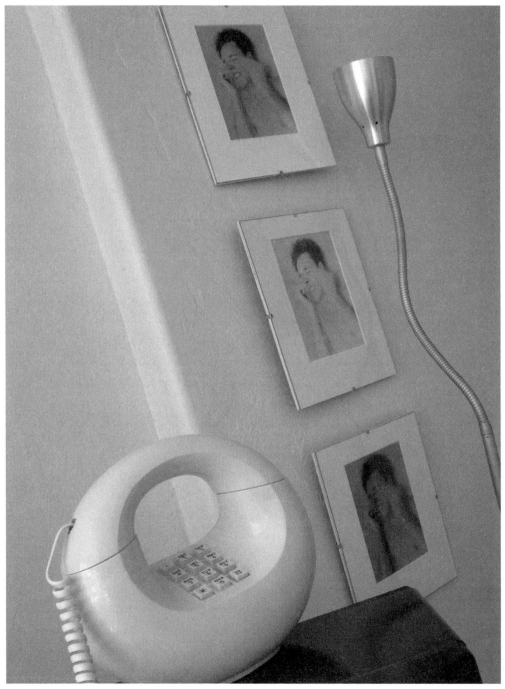

Clustering

some wall art. Low furniture placed against the wall generally benefits from the addition of some art just above, to add some vertical interest to the arrangement.

Use the colors in the artwork to accentuate colors in the room. It's a little anal-retentive, to be sure, and there is such a thing as going too far with the matching madness, but a little bit of color coordination between wall art and furnishings will do wonders for making both the art and the room look better. If you've decorated your room in cool muted tones, you may want to stick with artwork in a similar palette. Or if you've got a room painted in a snazzy ruby red, you may decide not to fight the boldness of the wall color with additional color, but to go with stark black-and-white images instead. Using colors effectively doesn't have to mean that your artwork matches your throw pillows; it just means that you should be aware of the effect that the colors in your pictures will have on their new surroundings, and vice versa.

Hang pictures in clusters. Grouping brings order and is especially useful when you're dealing with a bunch of smaller pictures. In general, it's a good idea to group together images that have a common theme or look. If you think you want to go eclectic, the key is to go all-out—randomness works best when you've got your walls jam-packed. Keep in mind that the space between pictures in a grouping should be much smaller than the widths of the pictures themselves.

Unify disparate pictures by framing them in identical frames. Got a hodgepodge of individual little pictures? The easiest way to tie them together is to use the same type of frame for each one. If replacing all your frames isn't in the budget, invest in a can of spray paint and coat each frame in the same finish.

Know the basics of good balance. Decorators are always talking about how crucial it is to find the "right" balance when it comes to arranging objects in a room. Which basically just means that you want things to look like they're sitting in the proper location—not too high, not too low, not too far left, not too far right. Hopelessly vague advice, no?

Fortunately, there are a few rules that generally hold true when it comes to finding balance in arranging pictures. Hanging pictures dead center on the wall often produces a strangely deadening effect. On a blank wall with no furniture against it, pictures will tend to look more balanced in that big empty space when you leave a little more space below the picture than above. Still another useful balance tip, passed along to me by an academic advisor when I was hanging a photo exhibition: You'll want more space between the edges of the walls and the pictures than between the pictures themselves.

Think about where a person needs to be to look at the picture properly. Eye level—or just above—is a sensible place to start, although there are definitely times when you'll want to go significantly higher or lower. A five-foot-tall painting needs space to be viewed properly, so you'll want to make sure that there's enough room for you to step back and take in the whole image. Likewise, a miniscule and exquisitely detailed pen-and-ink drawing demands that a person be able to get up close to examine it properly, so it would make no sense at all to place it high up above a deep armoire.

Work with the lighting. You don't want to hang your prized collection of black-and-white prints in an abysmally dark corner of your room where no one will be able to see it, right? Make sure your favorite wall art gets good light. At the same time, keep in mind that UV rays can cause a lot of damage to artwork over time. Color photographs and prints will slowly fade and change color if you place them smack dab on a wall that gets hit with strong sunlight; if you're dead-set on hanging your favorite color photo of yourself and the sweets opposite a big south-facing window, you'll need to invest in UV-protective glass for your frame.

White space is not always empty space. Unless you're going for the over-the-top kitsch look, don't be afraid of undecorated space. White space—the space between objects—helps emphasize the objects themselves. It plays as important a role in defining a room's focal points as do the pictures themselves. Your pictures need some breathing room; your eyes need an occasional rest. A little consciously planned-out white space is essential for creating that nebulous "balance" that distinguishes good decorating from bad.

Above all, trust your instincts. Read the rules. Understand the rules. Then feel free to break the rules. What looks awful in one space can look perfect in another. And if you get something up on the wall only to realize you hate it, no worries! Just pull it down, spackle the hole, and find a new place for your picture.

minor makeover miracles

O ccasionally I like to torture myself by flipping through the glossy pages of the latest issue of some schmancy home magazine. Page after page of expensively minimalist interior design will slowly, insidiously, poison my mind into the belief that the only way I'll ever achieve stylish living is by spending mountains of cash on a complete overhaul of my pad. Since I'm hardly swimming in the green stuff, I'm left feeling condemned to a shabby existence of mismatched futons and chipped secondhand end tables. Sure, those kinds of magazines can be great for stirring the imagination, giving you a glimpse of how other people live, and opening your mind to the possibilities, but it's important to realize that the way those folks fix house, in one grand sweeping makeover, isn't the only way to go about the process.

For most of us in the recent postcollege years, decorating our digs bears little resemblance to the knock-down-the-walls, tear-out-the-floors transformations that are generally featured in interior decorating tomes. Stuck in rental hell, we find ourselves living in abodes featuring teal carpeting and peach floral bathroom tile that we would never in a million years choose of our own free will. We dream of the day when our budgets will allow us to purchase a place of our very own, and we can paint the walls whatever funky color of the rainbow suits our fancy without incurring the wrath of our control-freak landlords. We fantasize about what we would do if we were the owners of this little apartment—how we would pick new kitchen cabinets, tear out the wall-to-wall carpeting to make room for hardwood floors, and replace the worn bathroom linoleum with fresh new tile. And while we wait for the day when we really can do whatever we want to our "nests," we make do with what we're given. Still, there's no need to just suck it up, accepting a blah apartment as your renter's fate. There are plenty of inexpensive temporary changes you can make to transform a less-than-ideal rental place into a space that you love.

Sure, every rental pad can be relied on to come with the basics: overhead lights in most rooms, cabinets in the kitchen, bathroom fitted out and ready to go. Sadly, these existing fixtures are typically ho-hum utilitarian at best, totally dated and beat up at the worst. No need to despair, however, as many of these things can be temporarily swapped out without a huge investment on your part. In replacing anything, of course, you should be sure to save the originals so that come moving time, you can return the apartment to its former landlord-friendly, characterless state and take your own fabulous fixtures with you.

the great cover-up

The vast majority of rental renovating is about covering up what's there. Since there's no point in spending big bucks making structural changes on a place you don't own, your primary goal is to find temporary, low-budget ways to mask any preexisting problems.

If your lease permits, or if a talk with your landlord gives you the go-ahead, paint can be a great, cheap solution to a plethora of apartment problems, including boring walls, ugly cabinets, and cheesy decorative bathroom tiles (learn more about painting in Chapter 8). But if there's no way you can paint without losing your security deposit, consider "wall-papering" your nest with fabric. There are basically two methods to cover your walls in a manner that will not make your landlord fume: stapling or starching fabric. Though both are removable, each takes a fair amount of patience, so if you're going to pseudo-wallpaper, do it in small, key areas. Choose one wall for instance, or stick with a border.

For stapling, attach the fabric at floor and ceiling level with a staple gun, using as few staples as you can get away with and still get the fabric to stay up. Depending upon the color and texture of your fabric, you might find the staples blend in just fine once you survey the finished results. But if those shiny metal bits are driving you to distraction, cover the staples with ribbon, fringe, decorative cording—whatever trim tickles your fancy.

Leery of adding too many holes to your walls? Opt for the starch method. Get yourself some liquid starch—not the aerosol starch, which isn't heavy-duty enough, but the kind that is meant to be poured. Tracking down liquid starch might be as easy as moseying over to your supermarket, but if you strike out there, try fabric and crafts stores, or hop online for a retailer. Once you've gathered the goods and are ready to start adhering, slather the starch onto the walls a little at a time using a sponge or paint roller, and gently smooth on the prewashed fabric. Come move-out time, just dampen the fabric and peel off, then wash the walls with some soapy water. With no trace left of your renovations, your landlord will never know you touched a thing.

Once you've taken care of your walls, it's time to address what lurks underfoot. Rental carpeting, after all, tends to range from the merely blah to the downright hideous. Hate your carpeting but think you can't do much about it? Think again: Area rugs are your friends. Just make sure to use a carpet pad to keep any area rugs from sliding around, or worse yet, transferring color to the original carpeting. And while a good rug generally doesn't come cheap, it can be a smart investment; unlike other flooring fixes, the rug can actually come with you when you're ready to move on to your next digs.

room-by-room renovating

For those of us for whom money actually is a major concern, home renovations just have to take place in more manageable increments, and on a much smaller scale. Knocking down walls, raising ceilings, and adding new rooms would undoubtedly do a smashing job toward jazzing up our apartments, but realistically speaking, these simply aren't doable options for your average recent college grad. Fortunately, there's a lot to be said for paying attention to the little things—making your changes bit by bit, room by room, one minor makeover at a time.

liven up your living room

For most of us, the vast majority of our waking hours at home will be spent in one single room: the living room. It's where we kick back to

watch a movie after work, where we hunker down with a good book on a rainy day, where we sit around the coffee table downing beers and sharing good times with the gang. It's the part of our apartment where most of our living actually takes place. Which means if you're only going to go through the effort of spiffing up one room in your entire abode, the living room should be your focus. Here are some suggestions for minor room modifications that can make a big difference in altering the overall feel of your living room.

Throw pillows

The throw down. Throw pillows and floor pillows are guaranteed to up the cozy factor of your living room. Add a few pillows to your sofas; stack some oversize floor cushions in a corner. In addition to giving you something soft to lean against when you're lazing on the couch, they're an easy, budget-friendly way to change a room's overall color scheme. Switch pillow covers and you can transform your room's look from bland neutral to vibrant exotic, hand-me-down tatty to chic and sleek. Wait for a good clearance and stock up on pillow forms at your favorite fabric store; as for fabrics, check remnant bins and thrift stores. And while pillows provide an easy way to add color and pattern to your room, don't forget to pay attention to the texture of the fabrics you choose as well. A good throw pillow should invite you to hug it against your belly when you're vegging in front of the television and to rest your face on it when you're sneaking a nap. So think soft, think touchable—go fuzzy with faux fur, silky with satin, cozy with corduroy.

Sofa savers. So you're still saving up for a real sofa and making do with your old college futon, your parents' hand-me-down seventies couch, perhaps. Yeah, it's not the sexiest seating in the world, but you've done your window-shopping and resigned yourself to waiting for that day when you can afford the couch of your dreams. In the meantime, don't just resign yourself to that eyesore: Dress up whatever seating you do have.

Futons are easy to outfit. You can buy futon covers at just about any store that sells futon mattresses. But hunting online will generally yield the best deals, and sewing your own cover is a fairly easy project that can be zipped off in the span of a Sunday afternoon (get the lowdown on how in Chapter 9). Sofas, with their curves and arms and sheer girth, present more of a challenge. The easiest fix is to drape a nice blanket over your tired-looking old sofa and hide it behind a mountain of pillows. But for slightly more effort, you can also craft a casual no-sew slipcover for your couch.

First, remove the cushions. Drape a big piece of cloth—a king-size sheet or tablecloth, for example, or a couple of sheets sewn together—over the frame, tucking it firmly into place around the arms. Hide the excess material underneath the couch, or use a staple gun to attach those loose ends to the bottom of the sofa frame. Now cover each cushion by wrapping it up with fabric (you can also group the bottom cushions and the top cushions as sets if you like). Use the same skills you've honed from years of wrapping gifts, but instead of taping up the parcel, you'll be securing the fabric with safety pins on the underside. Plop your wrapped cushions back into place on the frame, add some throw pillows, and you have yourself a brand-new couch.

True, if your style runs more toward sleek than slouchy, the sheet tactic might not work so well with your décor. If this is the case, try covering your couch with stretchy material—velvet with a touch of spandex, anyone? You'll follow the same technique as above, but the elasticity of your material should allow you to wrap the sofa much more snugly, provided you make liberal use of your staple gun to keep everything in place. And if all that wrapping and stapling is more work than you're really up for, you can buy slipcovers that will fit most standard-sized sofas. A new one will run around $100 or so—hardly chump change, but still heaps cheaper than a whole new piece of furniture. If you're going the ready-made slipcover route, check eBay first to see if you can score a better deal by purchasing secondhand.

Screen time. For hiding problem spots—a big metal monstrosity of a wall heater, for instance—folding screens work really well. They can also be used to create a little extra storage space. Just pop a screen in a corner, and stash as much junk as you like in that area behind it. And if you're lucky enough to be blessed with a great big open space for your living room, screens make excellent room dividers. Carve out a semiprivate little work nook for yourself behind a folding screen, or create a more intimate dining area.

Bye-bye blinds. Rental pads have an overwhelming tendency to feature those bland office-style miniblinds. They're perfectly functional but, let's face it, lacking in the personality department. If nosy neighbors aren't a problem, remove the window treatment altogether, stowing all the bits and pieces in a closet until it's time to move out. If naked windows aren't an option, though, you'll find that a little fabric can go a long way toward snazzing things up. Add some curtains: Even if you can't sew a lick, you can easily drape a pretty gauzy fabric over the existing blinds. If you want a curtain rod but don't want to put holes in the wall, try a tension rod,

Ditch blinds for curtains

though bear in mind that this works best for lighter fabrics. Curtains can also be used to cover up ugly walls—just add a curtain rod and some fabric, and you have an instant fix to warm up that cold cinder-block expanse.

Add some greenery to your scenery. Bring nature indoors—head to your local greenhouse and pick out a few potted houseplants. Plants have this amazing ability to add cheer to the dreariest of spaces—provided the plants look healthy and lush, of course. If you're adopting houseplants, you'll either have to make the commitment to be a proper caretaker to those lovely living things, or choose plants that require minimal care.

feed me, seymour: caring for your plants

The biggest potential problem for indoor plants is the issue of light. The artificial light you get from regular incandescent bulbs might serve you, a human being, just fine, but it's not going to do a whole lot for your little green housemates. Plants need sunlight, or a full-spectrum "grow" light that simulates the real thing. If you live in a windowless cave of an abode and you're trying to grow plants that require a decent amount of light to survive, invest in some grow lights. Head to your nearest DIY/hardware store and you should be able to find full-spectrum bulbs that can replace your regular incandescent bulbs in any of your already existing light sockets. Do be aware that too much light can be just as bad as not enough. The only houseplant I've ever killed was a devil's ivy—one of those supposedly unkillable plants that require very little water or other care. I placed it an area that got too much direct sunlight, and voila! A month later it had burned to a crisp, and into the trash it went. Make sure you do a little research to find out what sort of light conditions your plant prefers. Actually, the same is also true of humidity preferences—it *is* possible to kill a plant by giving it too much water. Essentially, the important thing to keep in mind is this: Think about where your plant normally grows in nature, because those are exactly the sort of conditions you'll want to replicate, as much as possible anyway, when you bring it into your home.

Add some plant life

Low-maintenance trailing plants like spider plants and devil's ivy are terrific on top of high bookcases, where there'll be plenty of room to let the vines hang down in a lovely curtain. Taller plants like ficus work well to fill out those corners of the room that so frequently go unused. And if you're willing to take on a little more responsibility, orchids make a gorgeous accent to any tabletop—if you're worried about your plant skills, choose one of the less fussy varieties, like phalenopsis (moth orchid).

Whatever plant you choose to bring into your space, don't just leave it in that dented black plastic pot that it probably came in. You don't necessarily have to repot your plant—that can be a hassle, and besides, you risk disturbing the roots. Just find a container that's slightly larger than your original, and you can slip the potted plant right in. If the decorative container is too high, spread some small rocks along the bottom to act as a little pedestal that'll raise the plant up. Basic red terra-cotta pots are lovely in and of themselves, of course, but you can also paint pots to match your décor.

better your bedroom

I don't care if you're in your office, in the library, at school, wherever. Close your eyes and imagine your bedroom. Not about how it looks, but how it makes you feel. If thinking about your bedroom doesn't make you want to retreat there right now, well, frankly, it's time for a makeover.

Your bedroom, more than any other room in your home, is a personal space. It's your nest, a private sanctuary; it's the one room in the house that

Creative bedding

guests—other than very special ones, that is (wink, wink, nudge, nudge)—generally aren't invited in to hang out and make themselves at home. Here's the place where you sleep, sleep with, and dream. Creating a great bedroom isn't so much about finding a fab set of furniture as it is about turning an ordinary, nondescript room—four walls, a closet, a door, some windows—into your personal haven. A good bedroom comforts you, soothes you, seduces you, and invites you in to escape the rest of the world. It's the most personal space in the whole house—or it should be, at any rate.

Feeling less than totally enamored of you bedroom these days? Better your bedroom with these quick fixes.

Beyond the bedding basics. The center of any bedroom is, of course, the bed. Which is why one of the easiest ways to give your bedroom a makeover is to get your bed a brand-new outfit. Outlet stores and department store sales are a good way to find bed linens at bargain prices. And if you're the crafty sort, flat bedsheets should be one of your project staples. Use them to make a new cover for your duvet or to whip up a set of pillowcases to match your sheets (it'll almost always be cheaper than buying the readymade versions); I'll give you a few sewing survival tips in Chapter 9. Fancy it all up with a pair of bolster pillows, or sew up some new covers for your throw pillows—use your decorative pillows to introduce a splash of snazzy new color into the bedroom, a sexy texture, a funky graphic print. You'll need so little material to cover a throw pillow or bolster that you can afford to splurge a little on a really fantastic fabric.

Heads up. Do something with that area above and behind your bed. Make a headboard by covering a big piece of plywood with some batting and fabric; hang a painting (get yourself some prestretched canvas, some paint, and try making one yourself); drape fabric to create a pseudo window effect. Heck, even just painting the wall in a strong, bold color (lease permitting) can do wonders for livening up the look of your room.

Light my fire. If the only light in your bedroom right now is that ugly old ceiling fixture that you inherited when you moved in to your abode, I have just one question: Why? Unless you have a thing for that particular sort of dim, dull light that standard-issue ceiling fixtures tend to cast, that light's not doing you any good. It's too weak to read by, too bright to be sexy, and pretty much unflattering to all skin tones, to boot. And given how easy it is to find funky old lamps for dirt-cheap prices at thrift stores, estate sales, flea markets, and the like, there's simply no reason in the world you should have to live with blah lighting. Get yourself a new pair of lamps for either side of your bed, hang a cluster of Japanese paper lamps over your bed, go retro with a funky swag lamp in the corner.

A better bedside. Forget the matchy-matchy bedroom set—there's no reason in the world your night table needs to look like it was born in the same factory as your bed. Heck, it doesn't have to have been born as a night table at all. Eclecticism makes for a far more fun look anyway—and is generally easier on the wallet. So get a little creative. Try a low bookshelf, a beautiful old wooden chair scored at your favorite flea market, an old trunk, painted in whatever crazy color you like, maybe even a stack of vintage suitcases. Or save floor space and install a small, wall-mounted shelf by your bedside. Basically, anything with a flat top at about bed level will serve you a-okay.

get a bitchin' kitchen

Truth be told, I could probably learn to live with a bad bathroom or a cramped bedroom, but an ugly kitchen? Just plain unacceptable. A good kitchen is a necessity of life, for anyone who spends any amount of time fussing over dinners and brunches, breakfasts and lunches. And if you're the social sort who loves nothing better than to invite your friends over every weekend, then you already know this fact: No matter how hard you try to lure them elsewhere, guests have a tendency to gravitate toward the kitchen. So for your own sake as well as that of your guests, do what you can to make that kitchen a welcoming space.

Sure, I understand, there are times when it seems like nothing short of a tear-out-the-cupboards full-scale renovation could possibly turn your bad-

fifties-era kitchen into something approaching an attractive space. And for most of us, a serious kitchen redo may be a nice dream, but nothing more. Still, don't just resign yourself to living with a kitchen you completely hate. Check out these ideas for small changes that can seriously spruce up your cooking space.

Get a handle on it. Change those cabinet knobs and drawer handles. This is something you can do even if you're renting—just be sure to save all the original hardware, and you can switch everything back to its former state once you're ready to move on to greener pastures. You'll find a gigantic array of options at any DIY or hardware store—just make sure you bring a drawer pull with you, so you can make sure that whatever you buy to replace the original will actually fit in the existing holes. Get rid of those old faux-brass drawer pulls and replace them with something sleek and matte stainless—you'll be surprised at what a difference new handles can make to bring your cabinets into the twenty-first century.

Top (with a) shelf. Add some open shelving wherever you've got some wall space to spare—next to the stove, above the countertops, by the kitchen table, wherever. Open shelving is easy to install and fairly inexpensive, and serves the dual function of looking nice (provided you keep the shelves well-organized) and helping to get all that crap off the countertops. Nice-looking brackets will make a big difference, so avoid those cheap, strictly utilitarian ones, if you can at all afford it. You can find reasonably priced, decorative shelf brackets in everything from wood to iron to cheerily painted glossy metal at Home Depot, Lowe's, IKEA, or the like.

Go undercover. Chances are slim that you'll be able to talk your landlord into replacing those hideously dated and beat-up Formica countertops. But if you're dealing with a relatively small area, consider getting a big piece of glass or Plexiglas cut to fit over your counter. You can now decorate your counters with pretty much anything you like—spray paint the glass and place the painted side facedown, wedge fabric between the glass and the countertop, arrange postcards, magazine clippings, recipes or other words or images beneath the glass.

Three-two-one contact. Hate that tile border lining your kitchen? Contact-paper it! This works best if you've got a somewhat funky, quirky look going on with your décor, since let's face it: There's nothing about contact paper that's going to make anyone confuse it with high design style. But it's an easy way to add some character to hideous tiles and banged-up laminate kitchen cupboards and drawers without going all-out to actually replace them. And unlike paint, contact paper's removable (although it's a good idea to test your surface in a small, inconspicuous area before you plunge into this project). So swathe your drawer fronts in a bright solid, or go with a sassy little checkerboard pattern border along your walls.

Extra kitchen shelving

Herbal Remedies. Grow a kitchen herb garden and you'll not only pep up your décor, but your cooking as well. Group a cluster of different potted herbs together for display in a sunny kitchen window—you can always install a little shelf if you don't have adequate ledge space.

bathe in beauty

Someday, perhaps, I'll find myself living in the perfect house, in which every wall, every fixture, every light switch has been chosen lovingly by yours truly and carefully placed just so. This, at least, is the fantasy. But in the here and now, decorating my digs is more about making do than about making things perfect. And nowhere is that more the case than in the bathroom, which like most bathrooms in the non–design-magazine world,

seems to consist of 90 percent items-I-can't-do-a-damn-thing about. There are the ancient built-in light fixtures that hang crooked and asymmetrical with respect to the mirror, which likewise sits cockeyed above the no-storage-space pedestal sink—we won't even get into the grotty bathtub, which no amount of scrubbing can ever render sparkling white again. So instead it's smaller changes I find myself making. Because even if you can't gut the bathroom and start from scratch, there are plenty of things you can still do to banish the blah from your bath space.

Theme it! There are some who will tell you that there's only one acceptable theme for bathroom décor: pristine and spalike. While the cool, crisp, and clean look is certainly a logical choice, it's not the only one. Basically, any theme that works for the rest of your house is a potential theme for the bathroom, and indeed bathrooms, since they tend to be rather small, offer the perfect opportunity to test-drive a crazy idea before you apply it to the entirety of your abode. After all, it takes a whole lot less effort to re-decorate one tiny bathroom than it does to retheme your whole apartment.

Of course, if you're renting your pad or are otherwise unable to make major bathroom changes, coming up with a theme or style may be simply a matter of making the most of what you're stuck with. Can't do anything about that salmon-pink tile? Embrace the hue and go all out with a fluffy-soft, rosy-hued, girly décor. Hate your sea-green toilet? Try an ocean theme and the blue-green toilet will fit right in.

Curtains up. Dump that nasty, mildew-ridden shower curtain that came with your pad. Head to your budget furnishings purveyor of choice and you'll find curtains in an amazing variety of colors and patterns. If you're feeling particularly crafty, you can also sew your own (just get a cheap plastic liner to waterproof things).

Throw in the towel. It's super anal-retentive and more than a little Martha, but one of the quickest color scheme changes you can make is to

the main theme

Theme decorating isn't for the timid; you have to be the sort of person who's able to embrace a semiarbitrary concept, then go all-out with evoking it to the fullest extent of your abilities. With theme decorating, there's no such thing as too much. A few ideas for inspiration:

Zen out. Bamboo matchstick blinds, accessories made from natural materials (natural fibers, unpainted wood, stone), orchids, and bonsai trees

Welcome to the jungle. Animal prints, viney plants, gauzy white curtains, mosquito netting

World traveler. Maps galore (framed on the wall, decoupaged onto storage boxes), postcards from exotic locales

Tiki heaven. Think tropical, think lush: grass skirts, faux flowers, dancing hula girl statuettes

Viva Las Vegas. Feather boa-trimmed curtains, sequined accessories, glitter galore, and all the bad Elvis art you can dredge up

Space age retro. Orb lighting fixtures; bold, saturated colors; graphic sixties and seventies prints

Even if full-on theme decorating is just a little more obsessive than you can handle, it's still a good idea to think about a general style and mood you're trying to evoke—bold and festive, sleek and modern, tranquil and classic. Doing so will help you narrow down the color scheme options. Look through decorating magazines and books; make a trip to the paint store to look at paint chips; get inspired.

swap your faded old towels for a new set. Color-coordinate it with a new bathmat, toothbrush holder, soap dish—you get the idea. Outlet stores are a great place to get good deals on new bath linens, and you'll be amazed at how much nicer your space looks with a brand-spanking-new set to replace those mismatched towels that were a carryover from your dorm days. Don't feel confined to boring old neutrals, either—

dress up the loo

In its original incarnation, the bathroom featured a border of country-quaint bath tile, along with a moldy white curtain that had seen better days. The floral tiles got a makeover with plain white contact paper. Meanwhile, swapping the old curtain for an inexpensive plastic bubble-graphic version gave the room a much-needed dose of character. A circular bathmat echoes the curtain's pattern, as does a kitschy disco ball. The result? A fun new look for the formerly prim and proper bath.

Before

After

sure, white goes with everything, but it can be a little stark, and there's nothing like a big sassy splash of bright color to add instant personality to a room.

Change the details. Toilet roll dispensers, towel racks, cabinet pulls, and toilet seat covers can all be replaced pretty easily. Make a trip to your favorite hardware store or home fix-up megastore and pick out a sleek new set of bathroom accessories to replace whatever dated hardware might have come with your digs.

Skirt the issue. Use sticky-back velcro to attach a skirt around the bottom of the sink basin, to hide exposed corroded plumbing and give you a storage nook at the same time.

You can go for a look that's just a little bit country with a cute gingham print. But a skirt doesn't have to be girly either: Choose a solid color, cool

Skirts for any occasion

stripes, or a bold abstract graphic, skip the gathers, and you'll have a chic, tailored version that's not froufrou at all. Of course, if you're going the kitschy route and have elected to turn your bathroom into tiki heaven, a grass skirt would make a fab cover-up.

Desperate measures. Sadly, of course, some bathrooms will still look less than presentable no matter what you do. At times like these, resort to lighting tricks. Replace your regular switch with a dimmer—nothing like keeping the lighting nice and low to hide all those flaws. In the same line of masquerade-it thinking, switch your bulbs to lower-wattage versions, or go with colored lightbulbs for a moodier, funkier feel. Naturally, if you use your bathroom for makeup application at all, it is still generally a good idea to have at least one set of reasonably bright white lights near the bathroom mirror, but there's no reason the overhead lighting needs to be glaring as well. When you're stuck with a room that's severely lacking in the finer details of good décor, the best tactic is to aim for ambience.

color me tolerable

Despite your best, most determined efforts, there will be times when you will find that as a renter, you've done as much as you can to fix up your pad in a manner that will still allow you to retrieve your deposit come moving time. That harvest gold kitchen or that mauve-tiled bathroom— these are the sort of interior decorating atrocities you just have to learn how to live with when you're renting. When faced with these sorts of situations, the best thing to do is to work with what you have.

Don't fight the harvest gold: Embrace it by going retro and collecting seventies kitsch. Remember, too, that colors look wildly different depending upon the other hues you pair with them—mauve on its own is pretty icky, but go over-the-top girly in different hues of pink and crimson and you'll find you have a really fun bathroom. Or pair it with a lively stem green for a fresh, cool, garden-inspired look. Love bright, bold colors but find yourself stuck with a mucky brown bathroom? Choose warm, rich earth tones with strong orange and red tones—a nice compromise between the colors you love best and the colors that you're stuck with as a renter.

Living in rental digs shouldn't have to mean holding off on your dreams of a swanky pad. After all, you may not be the owner, but this is still your home. So quit waiting until some far-off someday. Make it yours, one baby step of a change at a time.

variations on a theme of paint

When it comes to budget apartment makeovers, there's little that gives you more bang for your buck than a simple can of paint. A fresh coat of paint can work miracles on anything from that freebie old bookcase you inherited from your parents to your apartment walls. Still, that first time you walk into your friendly neighborhood home improvement store and find yourself staring dumbstruck down a never-ending aisle of paint can be enough to send you scurrying back home in intimidation. Relax: Painting isn't as scary as it seems. Here's everything the neophyte painter needs to know about the wide world of paint, including picking your paint, painting walls, painting furnishings, and exploring the virtues of spray paint.

on the wall

That bare wall: It mocks you. It stares at you every day from behind whatever pictures and bric-a-brac you've tacked up in an attempt to cover it. It's just so . . . plain. What it needs is some paint, but painting, you're convinced, is just far too much trouble. And besides, you're a renter.

If you're a dedicated, longish-term renter, however, painting a wall isn't out of the question. It's true that painting an entire room, no matter how small, can be more than a bit of a pain, but giving a few coats of sunshine yellow to a single wall is actually pretty easy—and can work wonders to transform an otherwise blah room into something pretty snazzy. One good color is sometimes all it takes to attract the eye away from milk-crate-dependent furniture and a smoker-phlegm-colored seventies carpet. All you need is the commitment to repainting thoroughly when you move. And in some places, Lord is it worth it.

I'm serious about the one-wall-at-a-time thing. Any more becomes a slow, painful lesson in the difficulties of multitasking, as this wall needs priming, but that one needs more spackling. One day, after years of therapy, I'll be able to recount the three-month battle that was the simultaneous kitchen and bathroom full repaint. In a studio. Where there's nowhere to hide. (Shudder.) Stick to one wall at a time, and you can work step by step, little by little, and moreover, you'll make it easier for yourself to back out with less agony, should your painting project somehow turn into a monumental disaster.

picking your paint

Once you've made the decision to paint, it's time to start looking at different types of paints. As this is a temporary installation, you'll want a latex paint as opposed to oil and alkyd, or anything else. Latex is cheaper, easier to work with, easier to clean up (no turpentine or mineral spirits required—just use good old soap and water), and easier to cover over once it comes time to repaint.

For your smaller, impermanent installations, the specific brand doesn't matter as much as the type and finish. Your average hardware store will carry an array of major name brands, like Glidden, Behr, or Dutch Boy;

paint stores often specialize (Benjamin Moore, Sherwin-Williams). For the label-obsessed, Ralph Lauren has his own paint line.

Brand name is definitely the way to go—not necessarily for quality of product, but for the availability of information and informed help that goes along with it. If your hardware store offers Grandma Margie's Generic House Paint avoid it, no matter how cute the cartoon granny on the label

the fine print

So like a good little tenant, you've read your rental agreement through and through, and noticed a pesky clause that expressly forbids you to paint your new abode. Still, you keep dreaming of adding some color to those standard-issue, dingy-white apartment walls. Quit wondering what if: Assuming your landlord's the rational sort, the best thing to do is just to ask for painting permission outright. Many landlords are actually okay with letting you paint your pad, as long as you tell them about your plans first. Your landlord might request that you stick with neutrals, and while this might not mesh with the kiwi green you were initially envisioning, you'll be surprised at how much better your room can look even in a tame hue like taupe. You can also allay potential fears of your landlord by making every assurance that you'll agree to repaint in a landlord-approved shade before vacating, or pay for a professional to do the job (if your landlord does demand a pro, however, think carefully about whether having those red bedroom walls is really worth the cost). Whatever you and your landlord decide, make sure to get the agreement in writing.

If you're pretty certain your landlord's going to nix your plans but you decide to go ahead with your painting unapproved, tread with extreme caution. Yes, you can and should repaint before you move out, but keep in mind that dark and bright walls are going to require a lot more work to return to their original pale shade than a more sedate hue. And be prepared: If any emergencies arise during your tenancy and your landlord needs to peek in, you might have to do a quick cover-up—either with a carefully closed door or a tacked-up sheet. If the potential to get evicted, sued, or otherwise screwed for breaking your contract sends you into regular anxiety attacks, axe the painting dreams and opt for other methods of pepping up your walls instead. Check out some ideas for decorating bare walls in Chapter 6, or try the fabric wallpapering methods outlined in Chapter 7.

is. The price range for brand name DIY interior house paint is around $17 to $25 per gallon. Outside of that, in either direction, and you'll be wasting your money.

Where you buy your paint doesn't matter all that much, in terms of actual paint quality. However, paint stores have the benefit of specializing in their product. The folks at, say, a Benjamin Moore–branded paint store will not only know their offerings inside and out and be able to tell you which paint products work together, but they'll also know a lot about painting itself. Specialty stores are great for getting tips, and their prices shouldn't run more than a buck or two more than Home Depot generica.

color me indecisive

As for picking a color, raid the paint counter for inspiration. Grab all the paint samples you can carry home with you, and tape them to the wall a few at a time. This gives you a chance to see the color according to the light it will actually be under, not those awful store fluorescents. Time now to play Paint Chip Thunderdome! Give all those paint chip contenders a good look when you walk by at random hours—check 'em out under daylight, lamps, whatever lighting situations you'll be dealing with. Start eliminating the chips a few at a time until a winner emerges.

As you're contemplating paint hues, keep a few things in mind. You want colors that lighten and highlight, that divide up space and make a place interesting. As it's only one wall (if you've been listening), a bizarre, eye-poppingly bright color can look really cool, without that overpowering I-still-see-it-when-I-close-my-eyes Oompa Loompa Land effect that might result if you painted an entire room in said shade. On the flip side, dark, heavy colors have a tendency to make spaces feel small and errors stick out, and will be harder to cover with white later on. Robin's-egg blue, lime green, nectarine orange = good. Crimson, navy, black = I warned you.

Need more color guidance? Here's a little ultrabasic color theory for you. There are two basic concepts in color choice—complementary and contrasting. Put simply, "same" and "different." For "same," you want a color that's a version of some color already in the room. It makes the object (let's

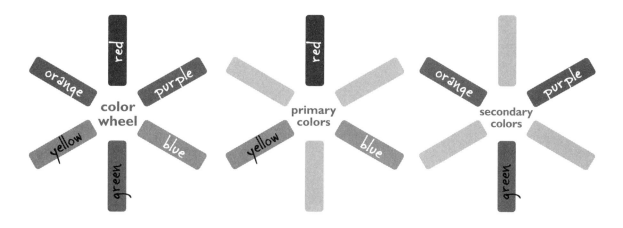

Use a color wheel as a starting point to find interesting color contrasts. Remember, you can always tone it down by choosing a lighter tint of a color. Violet and green might be too bold for your tastes, but lavender and pistachio, the paler shades of those colors, might be perfect.

say, my dark purple sofa) pop out while giving the room a cohesive, unified feel. It's easy to find colors in the "same" palette. Our friends the paint chips help us here. All the colors on a given paint chip are actually the same color in varying degrees. I find the paint chip with the same dark purple as my couch, I pick the light lavender on that same chip, and voila! For those of you without a solid color couch, use the couch's background color as the basis for your color scheme (or for the more adventurous, go with the second most obvious color in the upholstery print). As an example: Let's say your bedspread is beige with red flowers. Beige is your background color; green from the stems is the second most obvious color. Both are good places to start when trying to find that perfect paint color.

If you're going the "different" route, your options are pretty open. You're probably not as interested in making everything match as with making everything look really cool. To start with, get your hands on a color wheel. (You remember those from first grade, right? Red-orange-yellow-green-blue-purple?)

Using your color wheel, safe bets on color schemes are:

Totally complementary. Colors straight across each other on the color wheel provide the greatest contrast (red wall, green sofa, very vibrant).

All primary. Although it's my opinion that the red-yellow-blue color scheme was permanently ruined in the national psyche by Hot Dog on a Stick.

All secondary. Orange wall, purple sofa, very mod.

All color-wheel neighbors. Red wall, orange sofa, maybe with yellow picture frames. *¡Muy caliente!*

Of course, you can never go wrong with random earth tones. Neutrals are easy—they all go together.

An alternative to painting a whole wall is just painting the trim on doors and windows. It's a smaller job, uses less paint, requires far less prep time (you don't have to mask the whole room to death, or move as much furniture), and can have a great, subtle effect, especially in a small space like a bathroom. Here, dark colors and jewel tones look great. Sand wood to remove loose chunks; masking-tape the wall; and paint away. From blah to ta-da in an afternoon.

choose a finish

Paint comes in a variety of finishes: flat, eggshell, satin, semigloss, and high gloss. Flat or eggshell is what you probably have now. It's, you know, flat. (Eggshell is a little smoother to the touch than flat.) The other three finishes offer varying degrees of shininess: Satin is slick to the touch with just the slightest sheen, semigloss is a bit slicker and shinier, high gloss is very shiny and feels almost like plastic. (Because, well, it is. This is latex paint we're talking about, after all.)

Flat and eggshell are good for living rooms and bedrooms. The two glosses are best for kitchens and bathrooms (that plastic quality makes gloss finishes very easy to wipe clean—greasy fingerprints and the like just don't absorb as easily); satin is an either/or. If deciding between two glosses, the lesser of the two is the best bet. Besides, the less glossy, the easier to repaint.

Be aware that the finish you choose will have an effect on how you perceive your color—so there's a good chance that the color will look much different on your walls than in that paint chip. Higher gloss paints look lighter because of the shine, and most other finishes will make the color come out ever so slightly darker than what's printed on the chip. And this seems obvious: A whole wall of a color is different than a little card. Have the paint store check your mixed paint against the sample card before you leave. Even still, don't pitch a hissy fit if there's some minor difference.

With all that in mind, you're ready to head to the paint store, troops! Commence wall-contemplating, store-scouting, sample card accumulation, and that all-important Paint Chip Thunderdome.

get painting

So you've made the big decision to break with that ever-popular stark white asylum. With chosen paint chip in hand, it's time to do some paintin'!

Because there's so much prep work involved in painting, and it's so tempting to rush the job by painting first, then paying for it later in hours of cleaning and endless touch-ups, I strongly advise that you don't actually, physically buy the paint until 100 percent of the prepping is done. It's just too tempting to skip those important, albeit highly tedious, first steps.

protect your furniture

First, move all your furniture far, far out of your way. Cover it all with sheets . . . just in case.

spackle away

No, spackle isn't a popular Pennsylvania pork dish. No, it's not a crispy Hershey's product. Spackle is a putty for repairing walls. It's usually found near other repair odds-and-ends at a hardware store, in between nails and sandpaper. Spackling is easy, cheap, and makes you feel tough and industrial. Use a putty knife, tiny trowel, or very, very old butter knife to smooth on a tiny bit of spackle. Wait until it's dry (under an hour), then sand the area flat. If it doesn't work out, spackle some more. Spackle over all nail holes, dents, and that spot where your friend Andy kicked in the wall during that one party. For bigger holes, there are patch kits involving spackle and fiberglass mesh.

prep the surface

Next up, check for grease, weak paint, and stains. Your paint job is only as good as what's under it; if the old paint's peeling, your new layer will come right off with it. If there are grease smudges, the paint won't adhere properly. The standard test for peeling paint is the fingernail scratch test. No mark = OK. Comes off in a giant sheet = uh-oh. (Although, paint coming off in giant chunks can actually be a blessing in disguise—it means you can complain to the landlord and possibly strike a deal—you paint, they pay.) For paint with surface grease, marks, or mildew, give it a scrub with one part bleach to one part water; rinse well and let dry. For peeling paint, scrape everything loose and spackle *very* lightly over the ragged edge.

Vast tracts of spackled wall, or a slick, shiny base paint, require priming. Basically, primer is a slightly tougher version of paint, and the kind you'll need depends on what you're painting over and what with. Ask at a paint store and they'll help you determine what the proper primer will be for your project.

taping and tarping

Cheaper masking tape tends to have too much stick to it and will pull (old and new) paint off. Meanwhile, proper painter's tape costs four times as much (still not a lot, but it's the principle of the matter.) Get some of both, using the good stuff for right-next-to-the-paint work and the cheap stuff for grunt work (taping down newspapers, additional protection to clean walls, holding paint tray liners in place, replacing videotape labels). Flaws in the line between fancy colored paint and white walls will torment you if you're not careful in this stage. Tape the edge of the wall carefully, making sure the tape edge is even where it overlaps.

Cover the floor with newspapers and tape them down, section by section. Don't use sheets (they absorb paint too readily, staining the floor) or trash bags (they don't absorb paint at all, which means you'll inevitably step in dripped paint and track it everywhere). Pull off all fixtures that are screwed on (like outlet plates), and tape over everything else. Tape along the edges of the wall, plus two inches or so farther. Tape absolutely everything you don't want painted, and then some. This takes time. If you start getting bored and find yourself doing a halfhearted job, stop and come back to it. You'll thank me.

Okay! Now you're ready to . . .

buy your paint!

If you're keeping the project small, odds are that a quart of paint will be plenty. (For those of you who forget liquid measurements from eighth grade science, 1 quart = ¼ gallon). If this is a big job you're starting, paint a middle section of the wall, maybe one to two feet square, and leave it. Live with it a few days. Imagine the *whole wall* this color. If it works, continue. If not, start over.

Paint coverage is always an issue. On the can, they lie. They lie like dogs. Underestimating wall coverage is essential to ensure enough paint for touch-ups. Whatever numbers they state on the back of the can, figure it's actually half to two-thirds what they say. If in doubt, buy extra. It's far and away better to have a quarter can left over than to find yourself in a situation where you have half a wall drying while you haul ass to buy more paint—which you'll undoubtedly discover, once you bring it back home, doesn't quite match the first batch. At which point you'll also have tracked paint in your car.

putting paint to brush—but what kind?

First off, no matter what type of applicator you end up using for your paint, you'll need a paint tray. And a few plastic tray liners as well. Painting out of the can is a full-fledged disaster waiting to happen. (Unless, of course, your look is "uneven industrial art loft." Or you're only painting little stuff like trim.) First the brush doesn't fit in the can, and when it does, it gets too coated. Now the wall (and floor and ladder and can and you) are slathered in paint, which has lovely, even coverage on everything but the wall. Then you try to pick the can up, but it's got paint all over it, and you drop it. On the carpet.

Rollers are good for big spaces that have vast expanses to cover and plenty of room for you to work in. On small walls, however, rollers will only serve to drown the poor thing in paint, making the whole surface prone to flaking and chipping. Plus, rollers waste paint. In smaller spaces, brushes will probably work better. Brushes do leave streaks and uneven marks, but these can actually give the surface a nice textured effect. Nowhere is it written that walls *have* to be uniform in color and free of brush strokes.

Paint pads (those fuzzy, flat things with a handle on them) have the benefits and drawbacks of both brushes and rollers: good, generally even coverage, easy to use, but may need touch-ups and leave small brush marks. If you're a painting neophyte, paint pads may be the thing for you.

No matter what you choose to use to cover the majority of your wall, you'll need to grab a few smaller brushes (bristle or foam) for use on corners, edges, and other small spots.

start painting

Open the windows for ventilation. If painting up high, use a ladder and follow common ladder safety protocol (no leaning, no climbing to the top). If you don't have a ladder, and can't borrow one, use the sturdiest chair you have and get a friend to spot you. Now, starting at a corner, use your little brush or sponge-on-a-stick and paint *lightly* around the edges of the wall, following up with the pad or roller. The key word is *lightly.* Two or three thin coats look infinitely better and allow for fixing screw-ups. Besides, on the first coat the edges of the paint (where it's brushed on) will likely look darker than the rest. You probably won't need to edge on the next coat. Paint in a consistent direction, moving from dry spots into wet spots. Never put fresh paint next to paint that's already dry; it'll look uneven.

If you finish and spot brush marks where you started, leave them. Drying paint is sticky; going over it will create even worse brush marks. Subsequent coat(s) will easily take care of these imperfections.

Remove the masking tape *before* the paint is fully dry to prevent peeling and hard little edges. Be careful not to let the tape (which has wet paint on it) touch *anything.* Throw it away. Leave the newspapers in place until the paint is dry. Meanwhile, rinse out everything painty with warm, soapy water. Pour excess paint that's in the tray back into the can; squeeze out the roller or pad for extra paint (use your hands, it's kind of fun). Now go get a beer.

Paint becomes dry to the touch in a few hours, but doesn't fully harden for as long as two weeks, even longer in high humidity conditions. Give the wall at least a few days before doing a second coat.

Leftover paint that you don't want to keep around for emergencies should *not* be washed down the drain. Leave the can out to dry (somewhere away from kids and pets), and/or mix it into something absorbent (kitty litter's pretty good). If there's a lot of paint, try passing it on to someone else, either a friend or the scene shop at your local junior college's theater department. Or paint some furniture to match your new wall.

furniture facelifts

Paint is one of the best ways to make that hodgepodge of clashing hand-me-down furniture coexist in peaceful aesthetic harmony. Just give every paintable furnishing in your room a couple coats of the same lovely hue, and presto! You have yourself a matching set. A paint makeover is also an affordable way to brighten up that dark chest-of-drawers, hide the years of abuse on a thrift-shopped coffee table, or give those boring putty-colored file cabinets a hipper hue.

When painting furniture, use any interior paint you like. Bear in mind that matte finishes might look better in the short run, but tend to show dirt and wear more than their glossier relatives. If you're trying to balance your preference for a sleek flat finish with practical concerns, opt for a satin finish as a compromise.

Foam brushes tend to mask brush marks better than traditional bristle brushes, which makes them a good choice for painting smooth surfaces like metal. As for prepping before you paint, your first task will be to

the dukes of hazard test

After you've finished your painting project, you will inevitably see an error. No matter what that error may be, it can be solved by the Dukes of Hazard Test.

Step 1. Leave room.

Step 2. Watch a rerun of *The Dukes of Hazard* (or something similarly stupid).

Step 3. Return to room with eyes closed.

Step 4. Open eyes. You now have five seconds to find the blemish. Can't? Must not be important.

remove any hardware, cushions, or other embellishments that should remain pristine and paint-free. Lazy decorator that I am, I rarely bother with any primer, as I'm usually more concerned with a quick and cheap fix for my ugly furnishings than making sure the new finish looks gorgeous for decades to come. But if you're really concerned about paint longevity, a base coat of primer can help. And on very slick surfaces like plastic, a primer will help significantly in ensuring that your new paint job stays put.

Personally, I've found that wood and metal finishes in decent condition generally just need a good cleaning with a damp cloth, followed by a swipe with a dry cloth; with no further ado, the surface is ready to be painted. If the existing finish is badly chipped or flaking, however, a little bit of elbow grease is in order. Sandpaper the surface until it's relatively smooth, and then start laying on your color.

say it with spray paint

You pick up a groovy classic postcard on eBay for a buck—only to discover that the custom matting and framing that its odd size requires are going to cost you big. What's a girl or guy to do? With just a little information, a lot of inspiration, a ten-spot, and an hour or two, you're covered. Get yourself to a home improvement store and head for the spray paint.

Spray paint? But wait, you protest, you're not looking to write your name on a highway overpass in a personal style statement. Nor are you donning a hardhat and orange vest to mark things for destruction. So why on earth would you go to the spray-paint aisle?

Spray paint, you see, is the new *faux* faux-finish for people with little time and less money. If you haven't yet explored the wide world of spray paint, you'll be amazed at the range of possibilities that spray paint decorating offers. True, spray paint gives you a lot less paint for your buck than when you're dealing with good old-fashioned paint from a bucket. But with no paint that needs to be stirred up, no brush marks to worry about covering, and no fear of spillage, you can't beat spray paint for ease of use.

It's the ideal choice when you're looking to paint stuff like picture frames, lamp bases, even a little end table—small furnishings for which a whole bucket of paint would be way more than you need anyway.

At the spray paint section of your friendly local hardware store, you'll see the usual Day-Glo fluorescents, traditional paint colors, and spray primers. But did you know that you can also get spray paint that dries to a chalkboard finish? (And yes, it does work like the real thing.) There are also spray paints in metallic hues—chrome and gold as well as colored metallics, even hammered metals. Yes, that's right, folks: *hammered* metals. How an aerosol can of paint yields a surface that resembles hammered metal remains a mystery to me—but yes, truly, the stuff does work. There's also spray paint that can frost glass, or create a granite finish. And if you delve further into the spray-paint offerings, you'll find kits that can help you achieve finishes that mimic pewter, rust, copper patina, and even leather. These kits cost about ten dollars and take a little more work than a straightforward spray-paint job, but if you can afford it, go for the splurge! Personally, I've found myself tempted by the leather kit, but unfortunately my boy refuses to let me paint his car with it, despite my argument that his would be *the* most original finish in the parking lot.

But wait, you don't have a workshop! Spray paint is messy, right?

No workshop, no problem. Head outdoors. When you paint outside, you want to be cautious of the three W's: where, weather, and wind. Keep these factors in mind as you get ready to tackle your spray-painting project:

Where. Don't spray in the direction of any fixed object— for example, a house, car, fence, or tree. The farther away you are from a stationary object, the less the chance of spray residue getting where it shouldn't be. Also, be careful of the ground cover. For smaller objects, like picture frames, recycle a cardboard box and use it to protect your surroundings from paint. An empty box turned upside-down makes a handy tablelike space to paint anything that has sides, while placing flat objects inside the box works great to limit the residue risk. For larger objects, use a drop cloth to keep the ground paint-free. Whatever you do, don't paint indoors. A well-ventilated workshop area would work okay, but your windowless bathroom most definitely would not.

Weather. If you're painting outside, don't paint when it's raining. That's obvious, but if wet weather is predicted, make sure you have at least forty-five minutes of dry weather to allow the paint to dry properly. Also, humidity can cause paint to dry more slowly.

Wind. Paint in the direction of the wind. Instead of walking around the object as you paint, turn the object itself to reach all sides. If it's particularly windy and there is a high content of dust or grass in the air, painting the object in the cardboard box will reduce the chances of all that unwanted debris getting embedded into the paint as it dries.

One of the great things about spray paint is its cleanliness. As long as you follow the three W's, the only thing you *might* inadvertently get paint on is your index finger. If that's more messiness than you can handle, use some latex gloves, or pick up a spray can trigger at the home improvement store (about three dollars). For larger projects, I like a trigger, but for working on something like frames, I go commando.

The best thing about spray paint is that when you're done painting, there are no brushes to rinse, no paint to dispose of, no trays to clean. You don't even need to change into painting clothes—although I wouldn't recommend wearing your best formalwear, just in case.

Prep it for paint!. Spray paint is remarkably adhesive, especially when you use a primer first. But depending on the finish of the frame and how much abuse your painted object is likely to have to endure, primer isn't mandatory. Wood, for instance, generally takes paint just fine even without the primer, and objects that don't get brushed against much or otherwise jostled might be fine primer-free as well. To be on the safe side, though, priming is never a bad idea, and for small spray-paint projects, it won't require all that much more of your time. Primer will help with applying the finish coat in two ways: It provides a flat surface for the finish layer to adhere to, and it also takes out the shine from your original finish, making it easier to see where you've already painted, or where you need to apply more. This is especially helpful when working with metallics.

Cheap finishes and unvarnished surfaces generally don't require any sanding. If you're working with a very slick finish, however, you might want to sand it lightly with steel wool (for small areas and little nooks) or regular sandpaper (for larger, flattish areas). If you're in doubt, do a test. If the primer pools or separates from the old finish, rough up the surface with a little sanding first. Once the primer has dried, you're ready to . . .

Get creative. The aerosol nature of spray paint allows you to work with it differently than you'd work with traditional brush paint. The farther away you hold the nozzle from the frame, the lighter the coat. A light sweep of silver over a base color will add just a little sparkle (think hair glitter from eighth grade), while moving the can closer as you spray will produce a full metallic finish. For specialty paints (chalkboard, hammered metals, frosted glass) follow the instructions on the can if you want the results promised by the label, but don't feel limited. Experiment a little, and you'll quickly discover what works and what just doesn't.

For small-apartment dwellers, spray paints have the added bonus of requiring little storage space should you find yourself with surplus; a cardboard box under the sink is all you need, and the paint never leaks or dries up. With an assortment of spray paints in your decorating toolkit, you'll be able to give your goods a quickie makeover without breaking a sweat. Everyone will think you're Martha Stewart—they'll never know that all it took was ten minutes in your backyard and a press of the index finger.

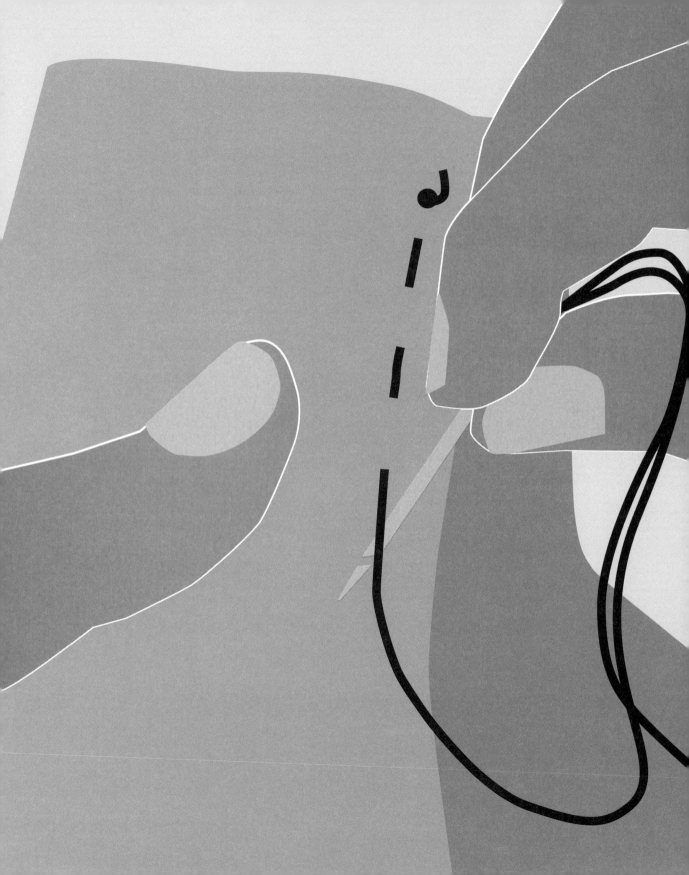

chapter nine

sew what?

’m sort of a hack when it comes to seamstress skills. Forget skirts, shirts, dresses, and the like—anything that involves much more than stitching together two pieces of fabric in a straight line is pretty much beyond the scope of my very meager abilities. So it never ceases to amaze me when I encounter otherwise highly capable quasi-adults who think I’m a genius because I can whip up some pillowcases. Those home ec classes we sat through back in middle school days—were they all for naught? Were we too busy passing intricately folded love notes to our boyfriends and girlfriends to pay attention the day we were supposed to learn how to sew a button?

Even if you never in your life plan to craft your own armchair slipcovers or haute couture knockoff, it pays to have a few sewing skills under your belt. You’ll save money and find your decorating options suddenly expanded. Get familiar with the old needle and thread and you’ll be able to create simple home goods that are not only custom-tailored to your needs, but guaranteed to be unique as well. Check out our guide to the sewing basics that every twenty-something guy and girl should know.

the essential sewing kit

Keep the following in the house at all times and you'll be prepared to mend pillowcases, reattach throw pillow buttons, hem curtains, and more.

* All-purpose (polyester or cotton-covered polyester) black thread

* All-purpose (polyester or cotton-covered polyester) white thread

* Sewing needles (buy a package with an assortment of different sizes)

* Straight pins

* Pin cushion (highly useful, but not truly essential; you can always keep your needles securely tucked into a piece of paper)

* Sharp scissors

* Iron and ironing board (naturally, you should already have these for, you know, the obvious purpose of rendering your clothes presentable to the world)

how to thread a needle

The task of getting a thin sliver of thread through the seemingly near-microscopic eye of a needle can verge on the maddening. A few tips to make the process a bit easier:

1. You'll want your thread to be about the length of your arm, unless you're really looking forward to getting all tangled up while you work. Cut the end of the thread at a forty-five-degree angle using the sharpest scissors you can get your grubby little hands on. (Actually, scratch the grubby; if you're sewing, your hands should be clean.)

2. Hold up the needle so that you can clearly see the eye. Make your attempt. If said attempt fails, wet the very end of the thread with just a tiny bit of spit to keep it from unraveling—no need to hock a loogie, though, as too much moisture will cause the thread to swell. Still can't get the dang thread through the eye? Take a little piece of stiff paper that's maybe an inch and half or so long, and narrow enough to be able to pass through the needle's eye. Fold it in half width-wise, encase the end of the thread within the fold, and push the paper through.

3. At this point, decide whether you want a doubled-up piece of thread or a single piece of thread. Choose the former for any situations requiring a very strong bond (buttons and other fasteners, for instance), the latter for most other situations. To double up, simply pull the two ends of the thread together until they're even. To make it one-ply, pull your thread through in such a way that you leave one side a little shorter than the other, and let that end dangle free.

4. Take the bottom (or bottoms, if you're doubling) of the thread, and bring it up to the needle. Holding the bottom in place against the needle, wrap the thread snugly around the needle four or five times. Gently slide the coiled bit down the needle and continue pulling it along the length of the thread until you get a nice, neat knot near the bottom.

three handy hand stitches

No need to become a needlework expert; with just three stitches in your sewing repertoire, you'll be sewing up a storm in no time. And here's a general stitching hint: You'll probably find it easier to work from right to left if you're a rightie, left to right if you're a leftie.

straight stitch

This is your basic, all-purpose stitch, used for any situation where you don't have to worry about a lot of pressure on the seam. The easy two steps are: 1. Bring the threaded needle up through the fabric and back down along the sewing line. 2. Continue in this pattern, pushing the needle in and out of the fabric at even increments.

A variation of this stitch, the running stitch, can be used to make gathers. Instead of pulling your needle all the way through the fabric for each stitch, take several stitches at a time and gather them up on the needle. As the needle fills up, gently push the fabric off the needle and onto the thread—instant gathers galore.

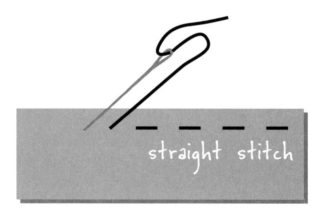

straight stitch

backstitch

Use this stitch for a sturdier bond:

1. Make a straight stitch for the first stitch.

2. For the second stitch, bring the needle back up through the fabric, like in the first step, but instead of pushing down the needle farther along the sewing line, make a stitch that closes the gap toward the preceding stitch.

3. Now, bring the needle up through the fabric, moving farther along the stitch line, at a distance that's twice the length of the stitch.

4. Repeat starting from Step 2 to continue stitching.

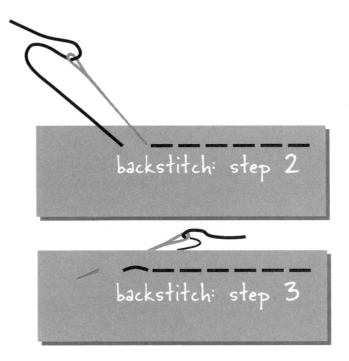

hemming stitch

Use this stitch for—you guessed it—hemming. With this stitch, you're actually making little diagonal stitches on either side of the line marked by the edge of the hem:

1. Hide the knot within the hem, and pull the threaded needle up through the hem. Moving farther along the sewing line, use the needle to gather a few threads of the fabric that lies just outside the hem, and pull the needle through gently. Keeping the gathered bits

of fabric small will help ensure a nice, nearly invisible stitch on the front side of the fabric.

2. Push the needle back down through the hem fold, but not all the way through to the front side of the fabric. Pull the needle out from under the fold.

3. To continue stitching, repeat.

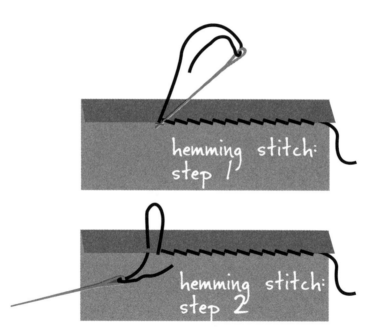

a-hem: how to hem

Granted, it's a lot easier to sew a hem with a sewing machine, but with small projects—shortening pants, mending the unraveled hem of your sheets, even whipping up a set of small curtains—you can hem by hand just fine. There's no need to throw away eight bucks at the tailor's; here's how to make those hems yourself.

1. Gently take apart the existing hem, if there is one, using a long needle or pin (there are also special seam ripper tools available) and sharp scissors. Be vigilant about pulling the thread up and away from the fabric before you snip—you don't want to be stuck with a big hole in your fabric.

2. Determine where you want to hem. Pin the hem in place. (Remember, you'll want to fold the hem inward, so that the excess fabric is on the inside/backside rather than showing.)

3. Iron the fabric to get a good, stiff crease. Snip off excess fabric, leaving at least 1" for the hem (it's a good idea to leave a wider hem if this is your first time hemming, it'll give you more room to work with in case you find you need to let out your hem line more).

4. Turn in the raw edge of the fabric ¼" to ½", and iron again. You should now have a neatly pressed, ready-to-go hem.

5. Start sewing, using the hemming stitch if you want an invisible hem, or the straight stitch if you're okay with seeing the hemline (as it's hard to sew a truly even straight stitch by hand, this is probably a good idea only if you're hemming on a machine).

button up

Buttons have a pesky tendency to leap off duvet covers, throw pillow covers, and the like. If you notice a missing button, try your best to locate it. If it's truly long gone, look around to see if there are any extra hidden buttons—store-bought buttoned goods sometimes have a spare button sewn into some tucked-away spot that's intended for just these sorts of emergencies. Still no luck? Head on over to a fabric store and look for a replacement button that most closely resembles the originals.

1. Remove the dangling threads from where the button has fallen off. Gently pull them out, using any sharp pointy object to help nudge them loose.

2. Use the holes left over from where the original button was sewn as a guide for where the replacement should go. If this doesn't work, pin the material together so the item looks like it's buttoned, and use the position of the buttonhole to determine where your button should sit; mark with a colored pencil and unpin before proceeding.

3. Thread the needle, doubling up the thread (which should match the color of the original as closely as possible) for extra strength. Give yourself 10" to 12" or so of doubled-up thread to work with. Tie a knot at the bottom.

4. Starting from the back of the fabric, near the holes for the original button, push your needle through to the front.

5. Pull the needle through one of the holes in the button, and slide the button down so it lies flat against the material. Bring the needle back down a different hole in the button and through the fabric as well, pulling it through until the thread is fairly taut. For a two-holed button, repeat this step a half-dozen times or so; for a four-holed button, make your stitches around two diagonal holes first, then repeat with the remaining two diagonal holes. This will form a neat X pattern on the button and give you the strongest bond.

6. On your last stitch, pull your needle through the buttonhole but *not* through the fabric. Firmly wind the thread three times or so around the stitches that have formed between the button and the fabric. This creates a spacer between the button and the material, and will allow the button to sit more comfortably when things are all buttoned up.

7. Pull the needle through the fabric. Secure the thread on the material's backside with a double knot, and snip the excess thread. Button up!

sew easy: buying a sewing machine

Sewing by hand has two distinct advantages: It's very cheap and requires little technical knowledge. But if you're attempting projects that are a bit more involved than, say, pillow covers, hand sewing can be a chore. If you're planning to sew new things for your abode on a regular basis, consider investing in a basic sewing machine.

There's no need to get anything terribly fancy. For the vast majority of household uses, you'll just need a machine that can do straight stitches and zigzags. Besides those two stitches, you might occasionally use the blind hem (for when you don't want a conspicuous hem line), reinforced straight stitch (forward three stitches and back two; this gives you the look of a regular straight stitch but with a little more stretch and reinforcement), and buttonhole. Any stitch capabilities beyond those five are almost certain to go unused for all eternity, so there's no point in paying more for a machine that boasts ten, twenty, or a gazillion different kinds of stitches.

Opinions on various brands and models vary widely, with European –machines tending to have a better reputation for reliability. But unless you'll be giving your machine some serious workouts, go with any of the long-established stalwarts (Bernina, Janome, Singer, Husqvarna Viking, Brother, Pfaff, just to name a few) and you'll have something that should serve you well for years to come—or at least be easily serviced if you run into any problems.

If you're buying new, the best place to get yourself a sewing machine is at a good fabric store or sewing machine dealer. The salespeople at these sorts of specialty shops should be able to answer your questions much better than someone at a department store or Costco-type establishment, and they'll have floor models available for you to test-drive as well. Best of all, sewing shops will often offer you a free lesson in how to use your newly purchased machine—which you should by all means take.

Bear in mind that the price you see is generally going to be the list price of the machine, and that these prices are sometimes negotiable. But if an attempt to haggle still doesn't yield a new sewing machine that fits your budget, you can also try going the refurbished or secondhand route. Try sewing machine repair shops (oddly enough, these often double as vacuum repair stores), many of which have good-quality used stock available from other customers who have upgraded. You can also find machines at yard sales and thrift stores, as well as on eBay, but as these sources generally offer no guarantee that your machine will actually function, only buy if you can get a very cheap price.

Whatever route you choose toward snagging a machine, it's a good idea to try the machine before you shell out any dough (if buying secondhand, this might not be possible, but it never hurts to ask). Bring your own material to run your test, and make sure that the machine is threaded with regular thread rather than something more heavy-duty. Stores sometimes try to cheat by demonstrating with an extra-stiff fabric that'll show off the machine's stitches to utmost perfection—while this is all well and good, what you really want to know is how the stitches look on normal fabric. If you think you'll be doing a fair amount of sewing on thicker material—upholstery fabric, for instance—ask the salesperson to put in an appropriately sized needle, and test the machine by sewing through a few layers of your fabric to make sure the motor's strong enough for the job.

Check that the stitches are straight and even on both the top and the bottom, that you can stitch in reverse easily, and that it's easy to wind the bobbin. If there's anything that looks funny, mention it to the salesperson. If a simple adjustment fixes the problem, great. If not, and the seller launches into some lame excuse for what the problem might be, try a different machine—and preferably a different shop, as well.

make this: a throw pillow cover

With your new machine, you're ready to start sewing! Pillow covers were the first things I ever learned to sew, so rest assured that they're among the easiest sewing projects you could possibly tackle. Check out our illustrated, step-by-step instructions for a very basic pillow cover—so simple you could actually create it sans machine if you wanted—along with some suggestions for (very) slightly more complicated variations. Here's what you'll need:

* Piece of fabric (W + 2") × (2 L + 4"),
  where W = pillow width; L = pillow length

* Matching all-purpose thread

* Sewing machine

* Colored pencil

* Measuring tape/yardstick

* Pair of scissors

1. Measure the length, L, and width, W, of the pillow to be covered. If you don't have any old throw pillows to cover, you can buy pillow forms (uncovered pillows) at any fabric or craft store.

2. Determine how much fabric you'll need, then hop over to your favorite fabric store and hunt down the perfect fabric. Buy a little more fabric than you expect you'll actually need, to accommodate for shrinking, bad measuring, unintentional spaz attacks, and the like.

3. Wash the fabric to preshrink, then cut to size.

4. Hem the short sides of the fabric by folding the frayed edge over ¼", then folding the fabric again (approximately another ¾"). Sew with a straight stitch.

Pillow cover: Step 4

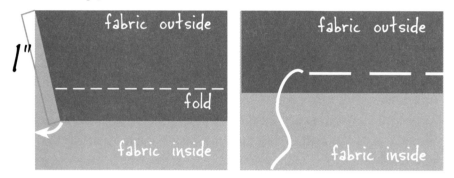

Pillow cover: Step 5

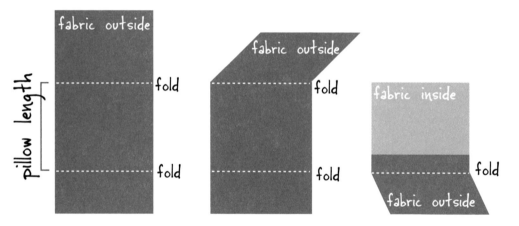

Pillow cover: Step 6

Pillow cover: Step 7

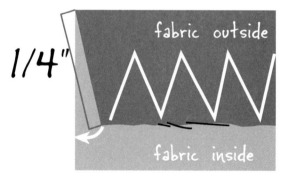

5. Place the fabric on a flat surface such that the outside ("right" side) of the fabric is showing. Make two folds in the fabric to create a sort of envelope, as pictured.

    It doesn't really matter where exactly you make the folds, although I like to have the first fold larger than the second, so that the cover opening will be near the bottom of the pillow. The important thing is to make sure that the distance between folds is the same as the length of the pillow.

6. Pin the fabric in place—this will prevent the material from sliding around while you work. Now stitch both sides shut, using a straight stitch and leaving a margin of 1" along the edges.

7. Now finish the frayed edges by folding them over approximately ¼" and using a zigzag stitch (you can use a straight stitch if you're sewing by hand).

8. Flip the cover right side out, and slide in your pillow. Voila! You're done.

variation: velcro-closure pillow cover

If your pillow is very fat, the simple envelope-style cover may not work so well, as your pillow innards will constantly be threatening to bust out. The easiest way to secure the cover is by using Velcro. In addition to the materials listed for the basic pillow cover, you'll need a strip of Velcro (both loop side and fuzzy side, of course) that's approximately $W - 4$" in length.

1. Follow Steps 1 to 4 for the simple pillow cover.

2. Place the fabric with the back side ("wrong" side) of the fabric facing up and with one of the short edges closest to you. Approximately ¾" from the top of the fabric, lay down one of the Velcro strips, and sew the strip securely into place. Fold the fabric as pictured on the following page.

Velcro-closure pillow cover: Step 2

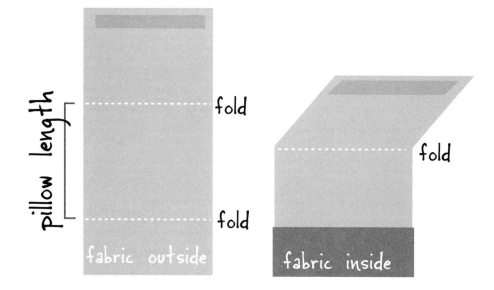

pillow length

fold

fold

fabric outside

fold

fabric inside

Velcro-closure pillow cover: Step 3

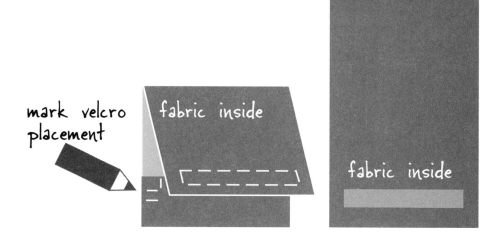

mark velcro placement

fabric inside

fabric inside

3. Mark the placement for the second Velcro strip using a colored pencil. Sew the strip securely into place, using a straight stitch around the edges.

4. Fasten the Velcro strips together, then flip the fabric inside out. Proceed to sew up the edges, as instructed in Steps 6 to 8 of the basic pillow cover instructions.

variation: button-closure pillow cover

The Velcro cover isn't so much pretty as it is functional; use buttons to close the pillow cover and your fasteners will serve double duty as decorative accents. You'll want at least two to three buttons for a standard sofa throw pillow (and even more for bigger cushions) to keep the opening shut. Follow the same instructions as for the basic pillow cover. At the end, though, you'll need to sew on your buttons and create buttonholes (this is the slightly tricky part).

How to sew a buttonhole:

1. Using a sharp pair of scissors, neatly snip your fabric to create an opening that is very slightly larger than the width of your button.

Sewing a buttonhole: Step 1

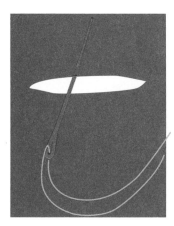
Step 2

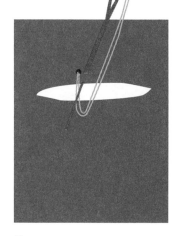
Step 3

2. Thread your needle, doubling over the thread and tying a large knot at the bottom. Holding the fabric with the right side facing you, bring the needle from the back of the fabric through to the front, inserting it approximately ¼" in from the opening in the fabric, as pictured.

3. Having pulled the thread through, your needle should now be coming out the front of the fabric. Insert the needle back through the fabric, going front to back this time. Now here's the important part: As you bring your needle through the fabric, you'll want to make sure that it goes *through* the looped part of the thread, as pictured.

4. Got it? Good. Now continue using this same stitching pattern until you've gone all the way around the perimeter of the buttonhole.

make this: a duvet cover

Tired of that boring navy duvet you've been using since your high school days? Give your bed a quick makeover by slipping your old duvet into a new cover. Buying one of these babies can easily cost a good $80 or more, but you can make one for a small fraction of that cost. All you'll need to buy are two flat sheets (look for good deals in outlet stores, or on sale at department stores) and some thread, as well as something to fasten the cover shut (Velcro strips, ribbon, buttons, snaps—your choice). When choosing sheets, don't buy the cheapo, low-thread count ones, especially if you're covering a patterned comforter. Higher-quality sheets will have a tighter weave and be more opaque. Darker colors will also be less apt to be see-through.

What you'll need:

* Two flat sheets (you'll need the sheets to be slightly larger than the dimensions of your duvet)

* Matching all-purpose thread

* Sewing machine (in theory you could attempt this project by hand, but given the size of the duvet cover, it's a good idea to get your hands on a machine if at all possible)

* Colored pencil

* Measuring tape/yardstick

* Pair of scissors

* Velcro strips, ribbon, buttons, snaps, or some other fasteners of your choice

1. Take apart all the seams on the two sheets. Tip: If you pull on the thread from the right direction, it should quite easily tear free from the fabric. To figure out which end to pull from, choose an arbitrary point along the middle of the length of the seam. Snip the thread. Try pulling in one direction; if there's resistance, give the other direction a shot.

2. Wash the sheets to preshrink. Iron flat.

3. Spread your sheets on a large, flat surface, most likely the floor. For each sheet, measure a length of L + 5" and a width of W + 2", where W is the width of your duvet and L is the length. Mark with a colored pencil, then cut carefully along the lines.

4. Take the finished (i.e., nonfraying) end of one sheet, and fold over $2\frac{1}{4}$". Using the straight stitch on the sewing machine, stitch along the width of the fabric. Repeat this step with the second sheet.

5. Place one sheet on the floor, outside ("right" side) up. Place the second sheet directly on top, back side ("wrong" side) facing up. Make sure to line up the hemmed bottom edges carefully (this is where your cover opening will be). Insert pins all along the perimeter to keep the two pieces of fabric together while you work.

Duvet cover: Step 3

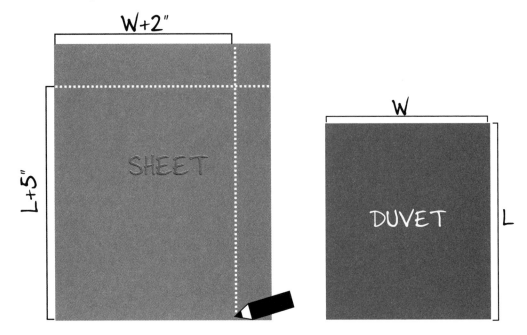

Duvet cover: Step 4

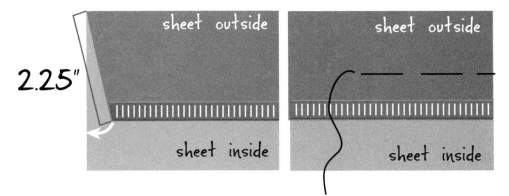

6. Using a ruler, mark ¾" in from the edge of the two long sides, and the unfinished short side. You'll want to use a T-square or L-square to avoid ending up with a lopsided trapezoid rather than a rectangle.

7. Using a sewing machine, sew a straight stitch to close up the three marked sides.

8. Almost done! All that's left is to decide upon a method of keeping the opening closed.

    If you just want something utilitarian and inconspicuous, sew strips of Velcro along both sides of the opening, or install snaps. For a prettier look, sew little strips of ribbon along the width of both sides of the opening to make ribbon tie closures. Or if you're up for a little more work, find some spiffy buttons. Sew the buttons along one side of the opening, then make corresponding buttonholes along the other side. Don't know how? Check out the instructions for sewing a buttonhole in the throw pillow how-to.

    Whatever fastener you end up choosing, you'll want to attach a fastener every 6–8"or so along the width of the opening.

Duvet cover: Step 7

9. With the finished cover turned right side out, slide in your duvet, adjust to fit, toss it on your bed, and snuggle up under your new covers.

get a little fancy . . .

Make a reversible duvet cover: Choose sheets of different color/pattern/fabric for the top and bottom, and you can make a duvet cover that's reversible to suit your mood. Choose a dark blue sheet and a light blue sheet; striped red sheet and solid red sheet; pistachio-green swirl sheet and pistachio-green dotted sheet; lavender satin sheet and lavender cotton sheet—you get the idea. Any closure besides the button closure (which has a definite front side and back side) would work fine.

make this: a futon cover

Store-bought futon covers are ludicrously overpriced. Rather than throwing your money away on one—which most probably isn't quite the shade you had in mind anyway—try making your own. Here's how to make a futon cover for the typical full-size mattress; for bigger mattresses, just get bigger sheets.

What you'll need:

* Two twin-size flat sheets

* Matching all-purpose thread

* Length of ¾"-width Velcro that's 5" shorter than the width of your futon (use black Velcro for dark-colored fabrics, white for light-colored ones)

* Sewing machine

* Colored pencil (in a color that will show up on your fabric)

* Measuring tape/yardstick

1. Take apart the seams on the sheets. Tip: If you pull on the thread from the right direction, it should quite easily tear free from the fabric. To figure out which end to pull from, choose an arbitrary point

Futon cover: Step 3

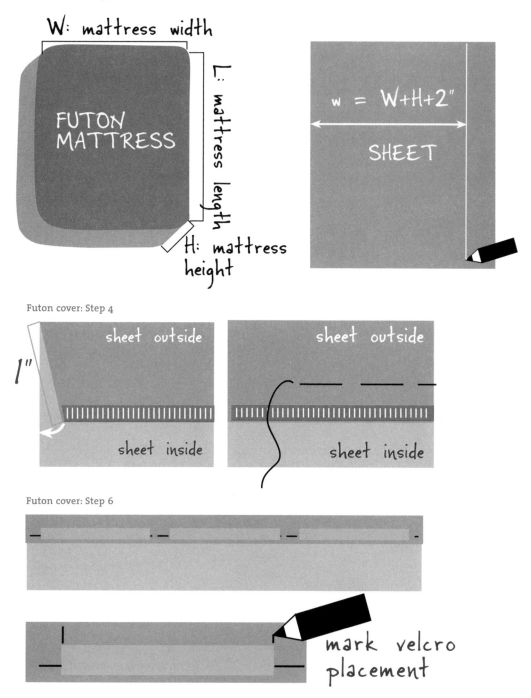

W: mattress width

FUTON MATTRESS

L: mattress length

H: mattress height

w = W+H+2"

SHEET

Futon cover: Step 4

sheet outside

1"

sheet inside

sheet outside

sheet inside

Futon cover: Step 6

mark velcro placement

along the middle of the length of the seam. Snip the thread. Try pulling in one direction; if there's resistance, give the other direction a shot.

2. Wash the sheets to preshrink.

3. Measure the length, width, and height of your futon mattress. For each sheet, measure a width, W, equal to W + H + 2", where W is the futon width and H is the futon height. Mark with the colored pencil. Cut.

4. Take the finished (i.e., nonfraying) end of one sheet, and fold over 1". Using the straight stitch on the sewing machine, stitch along the width of the fabric, leaving ½" or so at either end unstitched. Repeat this step with the second sheet.

5. Cut the Velcro lengths into thirds. (Tip: Stick the loop side and the fuzzy side together while cutting.)

6. Position the loop sides of the Velcro strips across sheet 1, leaving at least 1¼" at either side and in such a way that the strips are evenly spaced.

   Using the colored pencil, draw a line at the ends of each strip to mark placement.

7. Sew the strips into place using a straight stitch.

8. Align sheet 1 with sheet 2, as they'd be when joined (the "right" side/outside of both sheets should be facing up). Line up the fuzzy sides of the Velcro strips along sheet 2 in such a way that they match up with the strips on sheet 1.

   Mark the placement and sew with a straight stitch.

9. Line up the Velcro and fasten the two sheets together. Mark the length, L + H + 1½", and cut.

10. Turn the cover, still fastened, so that the sheets are inside out. Sew together the bottoms, 1½" from the edge. Sew up the sides (1" from

Futon cover: Step 8

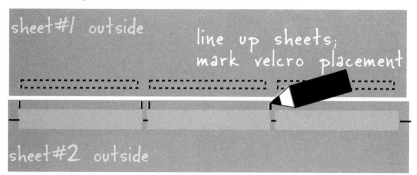

sheet#1 outside

line up sheets;
mark velcro placement

sheet#2 outside

Futon cover: Step 9

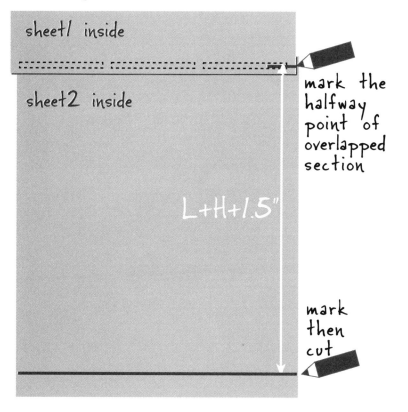

sheet1 inside

mark the
halfway
point of
overlapped
section

sheet2 inside

L+H+1.5"

mark
then
cut

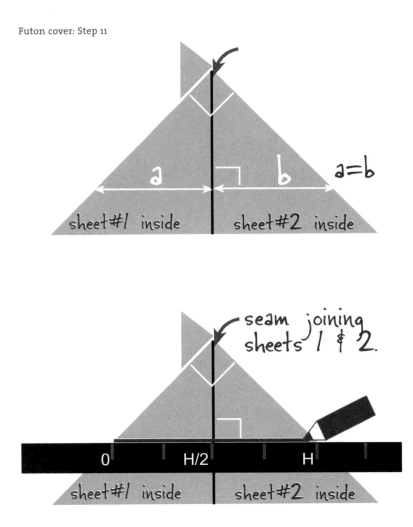

edge). Hem the unfinished edges by folding over ¼" and stitching a zigzag.

11. You now have two sheets stuck together to form a flat cover; time to form the sides of your cover and give it some depth.

Pick up any corner of the cover. Hold one sheet in your right hand and the other sheet in your left. Now pull each side of the cover out evenly to form an isosceles triangle at the corner.

Place a ruler such that the 0" mark is on one edge of the triangle, H/2 is at the seam, and H is at the opposite edge of the triangle.

Draw a line to mark the ruler's spot; sew along that line using a straight stitch. Repeat this step for the other three corners.

12. Turn the cover right side out and wiggle it over the mattress. Kick back on your new futon and admire your handiwork.

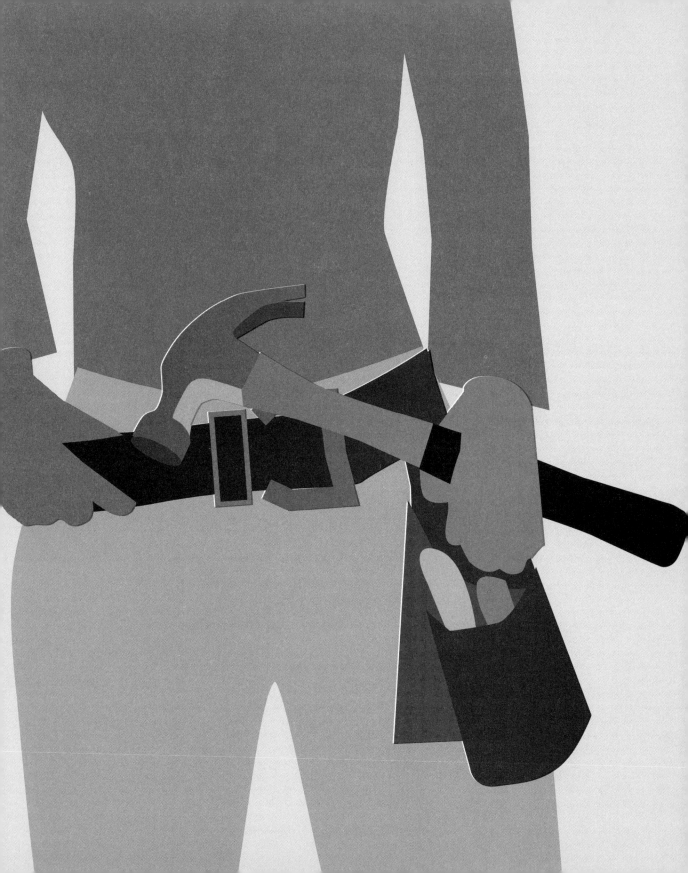

tooling around

i was a complete disaster in my middle school shop class, and, somewhere in the back of the closet at my parents' house, I still have the mangled hanging name sign to prove it. I had a pesky tendency to measure poorly and misalign; I could never bend the strips of metal to quite the right angle or get the screws to go in straight. Combining my mechanical inabilities with power tools proved to be scary indeed, as the tools would control me more often than the other way around, and I'd find myself with crooked cuts and inadvertent gouges—mostly in the wood and occasionally in the shop table, though never in my own tender skin, amazingly enough. At the time, it seemed a divine miracle that I managed to survive with all limbs intact, and that my kindly shop teacher decided to pass me despite my ineptitude so that I would never have to repeat the experience again.

As it turns out, however, my lack of intrinsic handywoman gifts is out-weighed by one deep-seated personal trait: I hate paying someone else for something I could potentially do myself. Once I realized that I could make, fix up, and repair things in my abode for far less money than it would cost to buy something ready-made or get a professional to do the job, I learned to get over those lingering insecurities from my days in middle school shop class. While I leave the really complicated woodworking projects to my much more talented boy, I'm no longer afraid of taking apart a broken lamp to fix it or picking up the electric drill to whip up some wall shelving.

So trust me when I tell you that even if you're not a handy type by nature, it pays to have a few very simple household tools and handyperson skills at your disposal. You'll save money because you'll actually be able to fix that wobbly chair instead of chucking it for a new one; you'll save face when you no longer have to call your buddies to come help you every time you want to hang a picture on the wall. There's no reason to be scared of tools, even the loud, powerful ones—provided you take a little time to learn how to use them properly, that is.

getting handy

Even if you have absolutely zero interest in ever building your own furniture, there are a few tools that will prove mighty useful when it comes to decorating, repairing, and maintaining your pad. This section explains what to stock in your toolbox.

screwdrivers

Ideally you'll want an assortment of flathead and Phillips head screwdrivers to cover a range of screw sizes; at the very minimum, get yourself a big and a small version of each kind. If you're short on storage space, you might also consider getting a screwdriver that has interchangeable bits, which can be stored in the screwdriver's handle.

Basic screwdriver technique. Screwdrivers might seem like a no-brainer, even for the tool-phobic, but it's amazing how many people are too lazy to use them properly. The most important thing is to choose the right screwdriver for your screw. Choose a size that fits the screw head—the tip of the screwdriver should be neither too loose nor too tight when it's inserted. And always use Phillips head screwdrivers with Phillips head screws (the ones with the cross rather than the single slot). Your screwdriver may slip if you try to make do with a flathead when you should really be using a

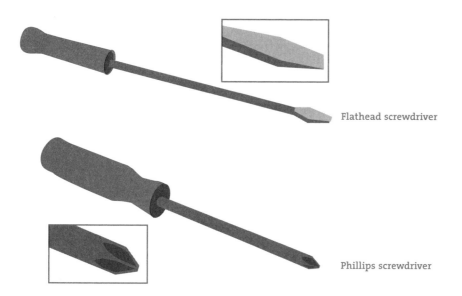

Flathead screwdriver

Phillips screwdriver

Phillips head, and this can potentially cause injury—or at the very least wreck your screws.

hammer

It's generally a good idea to buy quality hand tools, as the well-crafted ones really will last you a lifetime. Oftentimes, top brand names such as Craftsman will offer lifetime warranties. Splurging on professional quality, however, is probably overkill, unless for some reason you're planning to make use of your tools on a daily basis. However, with hammers in particular, avoid the real cheapos at all costs. The metal head of a low-end hammer can snap off from the wood handle, rendering your tool completely useless and possibly causing you bodily harm in the process. A 16-ounce carpenter's claw hammer is good for general household use. Give the hammer a few test swings at the store to make sure the grip feels comfortable.

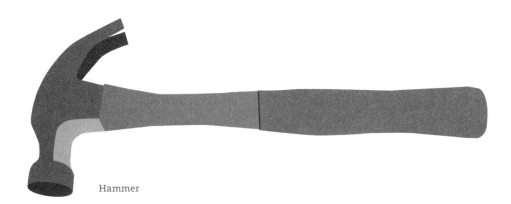

Hammer

Basic hammer technique. While it's hardly brain surgery, hammering isn't quite as simple as just picking up the hammer any which way and letting it swing. When holding the hammer, you'll find that holding it close to the head gives you more control, but holding it farther away ups the power. For small jobs like hammering a nail into that drywall, you're not going to need all that much force, which means you can wrap your fingers up closer to the head of the hammer; for driving nails smoothly into wood, you'll want more power, which means you'll want to hold that hammer closer to the end of the handle. Whatever you're hammering, remember to swing from your shoulder rather than from the wrist, and let the weight of the hammer do the work for you.

electric drill and drill bits

The big question you'll need to ask yourself when you decide to invest in a drill: corded or cordless? If you're going to be doing a lot of heavy-duty drilling, a corded drill gives you much more power. However, a cordless drill will be fine for most light household tasks and has the advantage of letting you move around without having to be attached to an outlet. For your typical apartment dweller, a cordless drill will probably serve you just fine, but do get something with a good amount of power, so you don't run out of juice midway through a job. The battery voltage indicates the power, and the higher the better—though sadly, this will also generally mean a heftier

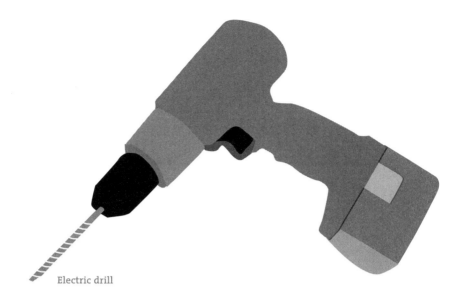

Electric drill

price. Get a ⅜-inch reversible variable speed drill with the highest voltage you can afford. As an added bonus, many electric drills also have screwdriver attachments that convert the tool into an electric screwdriver—which is why the reversible aspect is important, as it means you'll be able to unscrew.

Basic drill technique. If you're working with a corded drill, the first step is to make sure you've plugged that baby into an outlet that is close enough to where you're drilling that the cord will reach. If your drill's cordless, make sure the battery is fully juiced.

Choose an appropriate bit—that's the pointy thing that'll be forming the hole. Bits actually come in an astounding array of sizes and shapes, with specialized bits for drilling big holes, drilling in metal, drilling in glass, and more. Get yourself a set of four to six regular twist bits, which will work in wood and plastic (as well as drywall, though drywall will have a tendency to clog up the bits as you work, which means you'll have to stop from time to time to sweep away the accumulation). If your walls are concrete or brick, you might also want a couple of masonry/concrete bits (these also work well with drywall). If you're drilling to create holes for screws, choose a bit that's just a little smaller than your screw. If you need to create a hole of a certain depth, mark off the drill bit with a little bit of electrical tape so you know how far in to drill.

Follow the instructions that came with your specific drill to insert the bit into the chuck (the hole that holds the bit). Make sure the chuck is snug around the bit, and give the trigger a squeeze to make sure the drill is powered up. Now hold the drill so that the bit is at a ninety-degree angle to whatever surface you're trying to penetrate. With the drill on, carefully touch the tip to wherever you're trying to make a hole, and apply a gentle but steady pressure. When you've finished making your hole, keep the trigger on while you gently pull the bit back out.

adjustable wrench

For gripping, fastening, and unfastening nuts and bolts, an adjustable wrench will give you the most flexibility, as it can accommodate a variety of sizes. Get a big wrench as well as a small one. However, if space isn't an issue and you happen to stumble across socket, open-end, or box-end wrench sets at a yard sale, you might want to snatch them up. Set-width wrenches will often work better than adjustable varieties, since each wrench is designed to fit a specific nut/bolt size perfectly.

Basic wrench technique. Make sure the jaw of the wrench is seated properly, sitting flat and snug against the nut or bolt. If you have an adjustable wrench, you'll also want to make sure the fixed jaw is closer to you. Pull the wrench toward you while you work.

Adjustable wrench

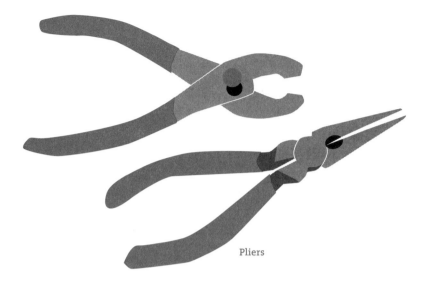

Pliers

needle-nose and regular slip-joint pliers

Use pliers for gripping objects and holding them in place while you work, as well as turning, twisting, or bending anything that's not meant to be handled by a wrench. You'll want both a regular set of pliers for heavier-duty jobs (like working with pipes and rods) as well as a narrow needle-nose sort for detail work (such as dealing with wires). Look for pliers with wire-cutting jaws and you'll get even more use out of your tool.

Basic pliers technique. Larger pliers will give you better leverage, so if you find you need more *oomph* in your twisting, switch to a bigger pair. Whatever sort of pliers you use, keep your wrists straight while you work and ply from your shoulder, pulling toward you rather than pushing away. And keep your fingers out of that area between the two arms of your pliers.

tape measure, twenty-five feet long

Whether it's for getting the dimensions of the living room in your new pad to find out whether that giant L-sofa is going to fit or measuring a length

Tape measure

of wood for shelving, a tape measure is an indispensable tool. Yeah, you might think you can manage just fine with that plastic ruler filched from your parents' place, but seriously, measuring large items is so much easier with a tape measure.

Basic tape measure technique. Just hook or butt the lip of the tape measure to one end of whatever you're measuring, and pull out the tape until it reaches the opposite end of the object or space. When you're ready to rewind the tape, try not to let the end slam into the casing, as this can loosen the lip and cause future measurements to be inaccurate.

utility knife

One little knife, a whole lot of uses—the utility knife is a household must. Buy a heavy-duty knife with a retractable blade (the latter feature is important as it will ensure that you don't reach into your toolbox and accidentally grab a sharp open blade).

Utility knife

Basic utility knife technique. To use, press and slide the button on the handle until the blade emerges. You can choose from a few different blade lengths; whichever you decide to go with, make sure the blade clicks into place before you start cutting.

level

No matter how good of an eye you think you might have, don't forgo a good level when you're setting up your toolbox. You'll pay for the omission later when you realize that your pictures hang crooked and all those shelves you so carefully installed are actually sitting at a slight slant. Get a 2' carpenter's level and you'll have something that works as a straightedge as well. Alternatively, you can go with the shorter torpedo-style level, which has the advantage of taking up less space and being handy for tight spaces.

Basic level technique. Just place your level on whatever surface you're measuring. When the little air bubble in the horizontal vial sits dead-center between the two center-most hairlines, your surface is perfectly level.

Level

saw

While the tools mentioned thus far are essentials for just about everyone, there's another tool you might consider adding: the saw. If all you need are a couple cuts of wood—to make shelves, for example—you can skip investing in saws and just pay the small fee to get your home improvement megastore to do the work for you. However, if you're hoping to make some simple furniture in the future, get yourself a hacksaw for cutting metal (pipes, table legs, etc.) and a handsaw (choose a combination saw, which will let you cut either with or against the grain) for cutting wood.

Eventually, if you find you're really getting into the handy thing and itching to tackle some bigger projects, you may want to invest in a circular saw, which will allow you to make cuts with a whole lot less effort.

Whatever kind of saw you're using, you'll need a sturdy platform on which to balance the wood you're planning to cut. If you're dealing with circular saws or other power saws, a workbench and/or some sawhorses will be essential. With handsaws, the work platform can be a little more makeshift if necessary. Co-opt an old table or a pair of stools to balance things while you work; basically, anything reasonably stable that gets whatever you're sawing off the ground should serve fine. One last bit of sawing technique you'll want to bear in mind: You'll lose a smidgen of width in the cut itself, so try to saw just to the outside of your marked line if you need your length to be precise.

Of course, the best way to build your handyperson skills is to put them to use. All set to start playing with tools? Get out your safety glasses, roll up those sleeves, tie back any loose hair, and try out one of these easy DIY projects . . .

make this: build a basic bookcase

I constantly feel like I'm running out of room to stash that beloved book collection, which between my grad student boy and my bookworm self, seems to expand at an exponential rate. Unfortunately, quality bookcases are outrageously expensive, and a good-sized one can set you back a few hundred dollars, easily more. Heck, even those flimsy white-veneered chipboard bookshelves—you know, the kind whose shelves start warping from the mere weight of paperbacks within a couple of months of use—cost a ridiculous $80 or so. Yes, I own one, too, but let's face it, they're cheap in every meaning of the word, and boy do they look it.

Fortunately, you don't have to be a trained carpenter to throw together a perfectly practical, though admittedly no-frills, bookcase. The best thing about making your own bookshelves is that you can custom-fit them to

Basic bookcase

your needs. Make a tall, skinny bookshelf for that unused little space over in the corner; put together a low, long one to go under a big window or your favorite artwork (it can also double up as a bench!).

One thing you will want to bear in mind is that books are heavy, and shelves will bend. Using expensive, hard woods rather than cheap, soft pine would, of course, reduce the warping problem, but there are other, more affordable solutions as well. First, keep tall bookshelves narrow and wide bookshelves short. If you need a whole wall of shelving, make several narrower bookshelves to fill that space rather than a single superwide one (or for an even simpler fix, install wall shelves). Secondly, you can flip each individual shelf from time to time to correct for the sag caused by the weight of the books.

Ready to start building? Here's what you'll need:

* 1" × 10" or 1" × 12" pine board, planed (i.e., don't get the unfinished, rough-looking stuff) and as straight and knot-free as possible. You can get your wood at a Home Depot–type place, but lumberyards will have nicer stuff. To calculate how much you'll need, you'll need to do a little math: Amount of wood needed = N (a − 1½") + 2a + 2b where a = length of bottom/top piece, b = length of side piece, and N = number of shelves desired

  Keep in mind that the longer a piece of wood you buy, the cheaper you'll be paying by foot, so it's less expensive to get one 12' section than two 6' sections. Before you begin, it's a good idea to draw out your plans for your bookcase on paper, approximately to scale, so you can figure out how to maximize your wood use.

* 8 1.5"-long countersunk woodscrews

* 16 × (number of shelves desired) ½"-long wood screws

* 4 × (number of shelves desired) L-brackets

* Wood glue

* Handsaw (or circular saw, if you've got one), electric drill, screwdriver, C-clamps, sandpaper, and ruler

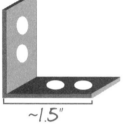

~1.5"
L-bracket

countersunk
woodscrew

1. You'll be cutting your pine board into two pieces of length a, and two of length b, plus however many shelves of (a − 1½") length that you'd like. Yes, that measurement for the shelves is indeed −1½", not 2", due to the fact that the thickness of your 1" × 10" or 1" × 12" will actually be ¾", not 1". Measure carefully before cutting, and mark with a line.

2. Use C-clamps to clamp the board to a pair of sawhorses or on a sturdy table/workbench in such a way that the cut line hangs just off the edge of whatever you're using as a support. You'll want to insert a piece of wood between the C-clamp and your board, to avoid putting a big dent in your nice wood. Using the handsaw, cut

Bookcase: Step 1

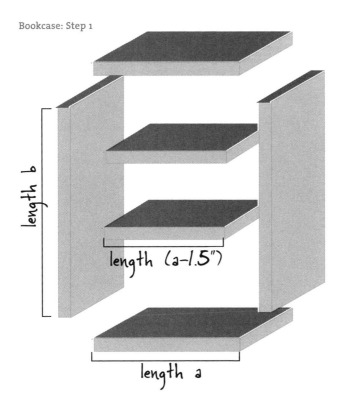

length b

length (a-1.5")

length a

Bookcase: Step 2

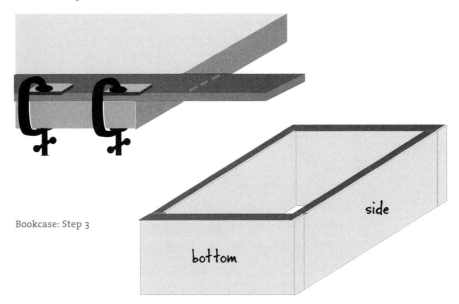

side

bottom

Bookcase: Step 3

the pine board with long, even strokes, following the marked lines as carefully as possible. Sand the rough-cut edges smooth.

3. Glue the two side sections to the bottom piece, as shown. Once the glue has dried, glue on the top piece. Let dry.

4. You're now ready to screw the boards together. Mark each corner of the top and bottom pieces of wood as shown.

5. Use a drill bit that's smaller in diameter than your wood screws to predrill holes where the screws will go (in handyperson parlance, these are known as pilot holes). This will help to prevent the wood from splitting when it comes time to put in the screws. Once you've drilled those holes, the screws are ready to go in. If your drill has an electric screwdriver attachment, by all means use it; otherwise, a good old-fashioned manual screwdriver will do just fine.

6. Determine where you want to place your shelves. Take a look at your book collection and determine whether you'll need tall shelves, medium shelves, short shelves, or a combination thereof. Bear in mind that it's a good idea to put the tall heavy books on the bottom, where there'll be no danger of shelf warpage. Using your ruler, measure along the two sides of the bookshelf to mark a line in each spot where you'll want to install a shelf.

7. Mount the L-brackets just under each line. You'll need two L-brackets on each side, one near the front of the bookcase, and one toward the back. Use the ½" screws to attach the brackets to the sides of the bookshelves. Of course, you can now stain, paint, or otherwise decorate your bookshelf however you see fit.

8. Slide in your shelves (painted and stained, if you'd like) so that they rest on the L-brackets.

At this point, you might find that your bookcase looks ready to go. But if things still seem a little rickety, you might want to make a few additions. If you've made a tall bookcase, you'll probably want to screw at least one of the middle shelves to the L-brackets to keep

Bookcase: Step 4

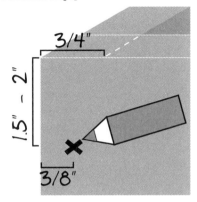

Bookcase: Step 7

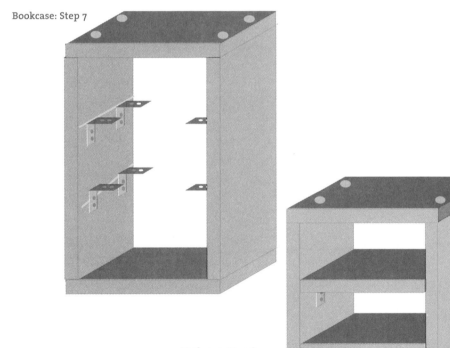

Bookcase: Step 8

get a little fancier

1. Add casters to the bottom to make it easier to move the bookcase around. This might be especially useful on low, wide bookshelves, which you could use as a sort of makeshift coffee table.

2. If you're dead-set on wider shelves, consider adding a 1" × 2" or 1" × 3" board that runs down the back of the bookcase. You can then screw L-brackets to that back spine, providing better support for the shelves.

3. Add a door or curtains to the front of the bookcase if you want to hide away any beat-up books from view.

the sides from bowing out. If you've made a wide bookcase and it seems wobbly, screw L-brackets into the bottom and top pieces as well as the shelves. You can also add braces (which look like flat Ls) to the back joints for increased stability, or alternatively, insert a vertical divider.

9. Add books and enjoy!

make this: easy corner shelves

The other day, I had an idea. It came to me from out of nowhere, a little cartoon lightbulb over my head. It was a tiny, tiny idea, but mine nonetheless, and when my boy came home that evening, I couldn't wait to tell him about it.

I'd figured out how to make rounded corner shelves. Cheaply and—here's the part that had me giving myself a big hearty pat on my own back—without any need of fancy, specialized tools.

Corner shelves are a terrific way to make efficient use of those frequently neglected little nooks where two walls meet. The weekend before I'd moseyed on over to Home Depot, intending to purchase a set of corner shelves for my home office, a first step toward getting my cluttered workspace under some semblance of control. To my dismay, I discovered that a basic corner shelf runs $18 or so. Now normally, I'm a big fan of just doing things myself, but here's the tricky thing about corner shelves: Since they look best when they're rounded—a little rectangular board stuck into a corner looks rather awkward—they're virtually impossible to make without the aid of a jigsaw (a power saw that's specifically intended to cut curves). Or so most do-it-yourself home improvement guides would have you believe.

Corner shelves

But then I had my brainstorm. Buy a 24" round board—the particleboard variety is fine—and cut it into quarters. That's it: four instant rounded corner shelves, which you can then paint in whatever color floats your boat. Easy, no? And incredibly affordable to boot. Check out the step-by-step illustrated instructions here. But first, here's what you'll need:

* 1 24" particleboard round (approx. $4)

* 4 8" × 10" shelf brackets*

* 4 6" × 8" shelf brackets*

* 24 #6 ¾" wall screws with plastic anchors (to screw into the walls; the screws should be labeled for masonry/hollow wall use)

* 24 #6 ½" screws (to screw into the boards)

* Paint

*If you're not putting lots of heavy things on your bookshelves, you can substitute the smaller 6" × 8" shelf brackets for the 8" × 10"s. Your brackets will then be nice and symmetrical.

As far as equipment, you can make do with no more than the following: wood saw, drill, straightedge/ruler and T-square, pencil, and screwdriver. Having access to a table saw (best) or circular saw will, however, make cutting the board a heck of a lot faster; an electric drill with screwdriver attachment will come in mighty handy as well. And as with most home improvement–type projects, it always helps to have a friend around who can hold up things against the wall while you check for placement and levelness.

cutting the board

1. Draw a line between any two points along the circumference of your circular board. To make Step 2 a little easier, make the length of the line a number that's easily divisible by two (I chose 20").

2. Using a T-square, draw a second line that evenly bisects the original line at a ninety-degree angle and extends from one edge of the circle to the other. The line you just drew will be the diameter of the circle.

3. Draw a third line that evenly bisects the one you just drew in Step 2, again at a ninety-degree angle. The circle should now be divided into more or less even quarters.

4. Cut the board into quarters, using a table saw (obviously the fastest, easiest option), a circular saw, or a handsaw.

5. You now have four lovely rounded corner shelves. Paint the boards whatever color suits your fancy. You'll need two to three coats of paint to cover the particleboard.

installing the shelves

1. Determine where you'll want your shelves to go on the wall. This is where it will help to have a friend around. While you're holding the shelf in place against the wall, get your pal to step back and verify

Corner shelves

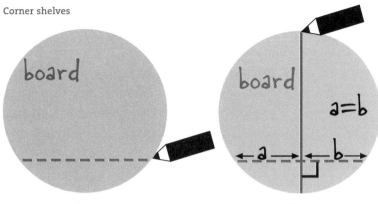

Step 1   Step 2

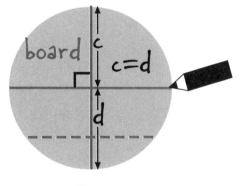

Step 3

that you've got the board level. You can use a level if you're so inclined—or if you're trying to do this project solo—but it isn't necessary; corner shelves, because they're so short, tend not to show slight slants quite as much as a normal, long shelf might. Once you've adjusted the shelf so that it's in the right place, mark where the bottom of the shelf hits the wall, using a pencil. Note: It's entirely likely that the shelf will not fit perfectly tightly into the corner—unless you've got a very poorly constructed set of walls, or you've done a truly slipshod job of cutting your board, you should be able to have at least one edge of the shelf flush against the wall, and the second sticking out just slightly. It'll look fine in the end, really.

2. Now it's time to determine where your brackets should go. Ideally, you'll want to anchor at least one bracket into a stud, of course. To look for studs, use a stud seeker (available at any hardware store), or rap along the wall until you hear the sound change from a hollow echoey sound to a dull thud. That having been said, it's entirely possible that you won't be able to find a stud under the area where the shelf has to go: What will probably happen is that you'll find that the only stud you'll find will be in the corner (studs are commonly found every 18", which means once you've found one under your 12" board, you're unlikely to find a second one that you can use). At any rate, in the event that you find yourself lacking a stud, never fear: You can put your brackets anywhere under that line you've drawn on the wall, as long as they: (1) aren't too close to the corner (you won't get good support); (2) don't overlap with one another. A good rule of thumb is to position your brackets approximately two-thirds of the length of the board, as measured from the corner.

3. Hold a bracket to the wall, with the longer arm of the bracket pressed against the wall and pointing toward the floor, while the second arm juts out from the wall and sits level with the placement line you drew earlier. Mark the bracket's wall position by penciling a dot in each of its screw holes. Repeat with the remaining brackets.

4. Set the brackets aside for now. Drill a hole at each point in the wall where a screw has to go. Use a drill bit that's just slightly smaller than the width of your screw—for #6 screws, that'll be a 3/16" bit. Make the holes just deep enough to accommodate the plastic anchors.

5. Once you've got your holes drilled, pop in those anchors, banging them gently with a hammer or other blunt object to help them go in.

6. Now you're ready to screw in your brackets to the wall. For each bracket, you'll have to line it up, as best you can, with the plastic-

filled holes. Don't panic if you find that your holes don't line up *exactly* right—as long as your screw goes somewhere into the plastic part, you'll be fine. Screw your brackets into place, using the ¾" screws that came with the plastic anchors—an electric screwdriver comes in handy, but you can do it by hand if you must.

7. Almost there now. Place the shelf on its brackets and, pressing down firmly on the top of the shelf while you work, use the ½" screws to attach the brackets to the bottom of the shelf. And voila—you've got yourself some corner shelves. If you want the brackets to blend in more with the walls, paint them in the same color as your walls (make sure you mask off the wall area before you start attacking those brackets with the brush). Otherwise, start filling up those shelves!

make this: picture hanging tracks

Blame it on my art student days, or on my sweetie's inability to say no to cheap, funky paintings glimpsed at too-frequent estate sale hunts—whatever the reason, we always seem to have more artwork than wall space in this nest of mine. To avoid riddling our walls with too many holes, we rigged up these makeshift gallery-style tracks instead, which let us hang as many pictures as we like without adding new nails. Made from materials that you can easily find at your friendly neighborhood home improvement megastore, these tracks can be installed quickly and easily, and are cheap to boot. Here's what you'll need:

* Strong fishing line or picture-hanging wire

* Picture hanging hooks

* ³⁄₃₂" or ¼" square cove cap molding. Home Depot carries these J-lipped aluminum strips, which come in six foot lengths. You can generally find them in the carpet edging section of the store, though

Picture hanging tracks

for some reason, every time I've asked for them by name, I'm met with a blank stare. If you're unable to find the molding, another option would be to use the tracks made for adjustable hanging shelf systems; shelf tracks will be a bit more expensive, but also sturdier, and they'll definitely be available at your friendly neighborhood home improvement store.

* Spray paint (optional—if you like the silver color, you won't need to paint)

* Screws (#6 ¾"), at least three per track (more if you're planning to hang heavy artwork)

* Plastic anchors to accommodate the above screws (Assuming you're installing the track in drywall; if you're installing in concrete, you'll need concrete anchors. If you're putting the screws into wood, on the other hand, you won't need anchors at all.)

* Electric drill

* Pencil

* Stepladder

* A friend

installing the wall tracks

1. Cut the track to fit your space, if necessary. (Tin snips serve just fine for this purpose.) Remember, there's no need to mount the track flush to the edges of the walls, since chances are pretty much nil that you'd be hanging your artwork that snugly to the edges anyway.

2. If you're happy with the silver color, fantastic—skip on to Step 3. On the other hand, if you'd like your track to blend into the walls, you'll need to do some painting now. Spray painting will be the fastest, easiest method—just make sure you raise the track up off the ground (stick a couple of bricks, tile, whatever underneath) and protect the area with either plenty of newspaper or a large drop cloth. Give it several coats (with white spray paint, I find it generally needs at least three or four).

3. Now it's time to determine how high to mount that track. I like to place tracks as close to the ceiling as possible, to make them less conspicuous, but the choice is up to you—you could certainly position them lower if you're vertically challenged and don't want to go to the bother of dragging out a ladder or stepstool every time you need to change the artwork. Two things to keep in mind: 1. The track should obviously be positioned higher than the tops of whatever artwork you'll eventually hang, and 2. leave an inch or so above the track so you're not bonking your knuckles against the ceiling when it's time to hang or move a picture.

4. Still holding that track in position? Good. You'll notice that there are little holes distributed all over the track—choose one hole each about 3" to 6" in from both ends (closer to 3" for shorter tracks, toward 6" for longer tracks), plus a third hole in the center; mark the positions of all three holes with a pencil. (As mentioned in the materials section, mark extra holes if you're planning to hang heavy artwork and want extra screws for greater support.)

5. Arms tired? Set the track aside for now. Drill a hole at each pencil mark. (Make sure to use a drill bit that's an appropriate size for your plastic anchors and screws. If you're using anchors, use the drill bit suggested on the anchor package.)

6. Gently hammer in the anchors, if you're using them.

7. Hoist the track back up into place again. Line it up with the holes you've drilled/the anchors you've hammered in. Get a friend to help hold up the runner for you while you screw it into place.

hanging pictures from your snazzy new tracks

If your picture frame has attachments on all four sides of the frame's backside, just thread the fishing line or wire through on both sides of the picture.

Alternatively, you can use two picture hanging hooks, slipping them under the top lip of the back of the frame.

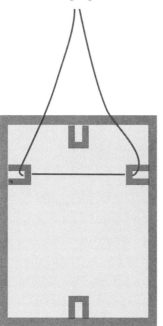

Preparing picture for hanging

Once you've threaded the fishing line or hanging wire, slip on one of the picture-hanging hooks, then bring the two ends of the line together. Determine the length of line—while supporting the bottom of the picture frame with one hand, hold the two ends of the line with your other hand and place the picture against the wall at the desired height. Raise the hand that holds the fishing line until it touches the track, allowing the fishing line to tighten or slacken as necessary. This will tell you where to tie your knot.

Tie a firm knot, then tie another one in the same place. Hang the picture-hanging hook on the lip of the track, then step back to take a look. If your picture frame is fairly heavy, it'll probably pull the fishing line/hanging wire down farther than you anticipated; at this point, you can eyeball how much higher you'll need to take in the length of fishing line, and adjust accordingly. Once you've decided you've found the perfect height, knot the line three or four times and pop the picture hook back on the track. Now stand back, admire your handiwork, and enjoy your own private little art exhibition in the comfort of your own home.

chapter eleven

the lazy decorator's bag of tricks

Walk into my current bedroom, and you'll see a window flanked by a pair of silky, chocolatey-brown curtains. They give the room a warm, cozy feel and provide a sort of frame to set off my bed. But mostly, they serve to hide my dingy off-white textured apartment wall. My curtains, dare I say it, look pretty darn nice. But here's a little secret: Get up close to the curtains, and you may well discover that they're nothing more than two panels of polyester lining fabric, not even hemmed, carefully gathered and secured into place using a combination of staples and binder clips. Yes folks, I crafted my curtains with office supplies.

Sure, the perfectionist in me is always chiding that if you're going to do something at all, do it well. But doing it well frequently translates into a huge investment of time and energy, and when it comes to decorating your cozy little nest, a fair amount of money, as well. In the case of my faux curtains, I saw no point in fussing with real gathered curtains or splurging on luxe fabric when I knew I'd be leaving this apartment in just a year and a half, and have every intention of moving with as little junk as possible. These are temporary curtains, a makeshift solution, a way to make my current pad look a little nicer without having to get terribly invested in the process.

The reality for most of us is that we occasionally have to just make do—and indeed, there are times when those quick, easy, somewhat temporary fixes just make more sense given how often and how quickly our living situations seem to change in the postcollege years. Why bother sanding, staining, and refinishing that hand-me-down dining table set when you're just using it until you've saved up enough to buy a replacement you genuinely like? Why give that lumpy old office chair a proper reupholstering when it was a freebie you snagged from the street corner on junk day, and you have no intention of bringing it with you when you move cross-country for grad school next fall? When you haven't spent a lot of money on your furnishings in the first place and when you have no intention of holding on to them for years down the line, you don't want to be spending fat wads of cash on rendering them usable, or giving up too much of your precious free time. Still, making do should never have to mean sacrificing style. Fortunately with the right tools and materials, no one will even suspect you took the lazy way out.

getting started with makeshift improvements

Yes, while sewing is a very handy skill and no quasi-adult's pad should be without a few basic tools, there are times when you might not want to go through the effort of fixing things up the proper way, and opt for a few smart shortcuts instead. Most of these shortcuts aren't meant to provide long-term solutions for your décor, but they come in mighty handy when you're in the market for a fast and painless fix for many a décor dilemma. Here are nine little tricks that every budding decorator will want to know about.

shoot 'em up . . . with a staple gun

Need a quick facelift for that truly grotesque set of free dining chairs you inherited from your aunt—you know, the ones with the oh-so-unhip horse motif upholstery? Have a great, big piece of so-hideous-it's-cool seventies-era fabric that you're just dying to attach to a wooden frame to use as a wall hanging? Or maybe you're itching to cover your dull white walls in floor-to-ceiling burlap but can't for the life of you figure out how to attach it? I have five simple words of advice for you, my friend: Get yourself a staple gun. If hard-pressed, of course, you might be able to make do with your dinky office stapler, but I guarantee that the staples won't go in as smoothly and you won't be able to work as quickly as if you'd just gone out and bought yourself a decent staple gun. Manual staple guns of the squeeze-trigger sort are available at both craft stores and hardware stores, in both light-duty (fine for most craft projects and light upholstery projects) and heavy-duty versions (better for serious reupholstering and home repairs).

fasten up—with velcro

Hand-sewing buttons and buttonholes is often more work than I feel like expending, and I still can't figure out how to install a zipper properly. So when it comes to finding a way to close up those duvet covers, throw pillow covers, and futon covers, Velcro is the big winner in that competition for fastener of choice. For projects like these, I love sew-on Velcro, since it takes about two minutes to attach using my sewing machine and stands up well to repeated washings in the laundry machine. In fact, there's only one fastener that beats sew-on Velcro for laze appeal—sticky-back Velcro. This genius invention requires you to do little more than peel off the adhesive backing on both sides of the Velcro and slap each piece of Velcro into place. Self-adhesive Velcro can be used in just about any project where you don't have to worry about washability issues. Use it to attach wall hangings when you can't drill holes, attach a fabric curtain to hide your messy bookcase shelves, or make a skirt to camouflage the exposed pipes of your bathroom sink.

it's (no) sew simple: no-sew tape

You don't need a sewing machine, or even a needle and thread, to make tablecloths, curtains, and other fabric goods. No-sew tape is a miraculous gauzy white tape that allows you to bond fabric using just the heat of an iron. The result is both fully flexible as well as washable. Perfect for making hems sans sewing machine, no-sew tape can also be used to add little decorative touches, like ribbon trim, to your decorating projects. Stitch Witchery is the most common brand and should be available at your friendly neighborhood fabric store.

hot stuff: the hot glue gun

Nails, screws, and even staples can do a good job of securing flat objects together, but when you don't want a visible fastener or are working with curves, what's a lazy decorator to do? In many an instance, the hot glue gun just may be your savior. It works fast and generates way less mess than wrestling with a bottle of Elmer's. Make a lampshade new by glue-gunning funky fabric to it; add some texture to those picture frames by adhering marbles, pennies, Super Balls—whatever little doodads tickle your fancy; turn those cheapo party favors into magnets for your fridge. The hot glue gun is the crafty girl or guy's best friend. But please, do be careful: Because it *is,* you know, *hot.* The hot glue gun is such a cinch to use that it's easy to delude yourself into thinking you can watch your favorite TV show and hot glue at the same time. But a tiny droplet of sizzling-hot melty glue can inflict a nasty burn, indeed; find your eyes distracted for just a second and I guarantee that's when the glue will decide it's time to say hello to your tender skin. So pay attention while you work. You have been warned.

it's a tablecloth! it's a curtain! no . . . it's a bedsheet!

The flat bedsheet's decorating potential extends far beyond its intended purpose as a mattress covering. Because it's basically the biggest continuous piece of fabric you'll be able to find, using sheets in fabric decorating projects will often save you the effort of having to piece together narrower widths the way you'd have to if you were working with fabric from a bolt. Use bedsheets for window curtains, shower curtains, pillowcases (it's so much cheaper to make your own standard-size pillowcases out of a flat sheet than to buy pillowcases ready-made), futon covers, duvet covers, sofa cover-ups, tablecloths—just about any instance where you need large swathes of fabric. Sheets come in a wide array of colors and all sorts of patterns, and can be snagged cheaply at both discount home goods shops and outlet stores. Keep an eye out for them in the clearance sections for the best deals.

go undercover: self-adhesive cord cover

Between your TV, DVD, and stereo components, telephone and modem, computer, and other peripherals, your apartment is likely to be a chaotic jumble of cords snaking here, there, and everywhere, threatening to trip you up and looking mighty ugly all at the same time. If money were no object and you actually owned your abode, you could, of course, tear out the walls and ceilings and hide all the unsightly wires within. For those of us for whom budgets and lease restrictions are an issue, however, fret not: There's self-adhesive cord cover, available at any DIY store. Hide messy cords with this fantastic little creation, essentially a white plastic tube that lets you slip your wire inside it, then tack it to the walls, along the floor, the ceiling, wherever. You can cut cord cover to whatever length you desire, paint it to match the walls, and buy L-joints to make your wire run neatly along corners. Granted, it's not quite as versatile a decorating item as the staple gun or glue gun, but in this technology-dependent age in which we live, self-adhesive cord cover is a decorating essential.

roll with it: casters

When was the last time you rearranged a room in your current digs? A full-scale, move-all-the-furniture-around rearranging, that is? More likely than not, you put the sofa against the wall and the TV in the corner and the bed by the window when you first moved in—and everything's pretty much stayed put in the time that's elapsed since then. TV stands, beds, bookcases—those suckers are heavy, and moving them is just more effort than you, the lazy decorator, is willing to invest, right? That is, unless you've had the foresight to attach casters to your furnishings! Casters render even the most unwieldy furniture mobile, allowing you to shuffle your stuff around without breaking a sweat. You'll find that once your furniture goes mobile, you'll be able to make much better use of your space, sliding furnishings out of the way when you don't need them, and back into place when you do.

grrrrrrrr-ommets!

Say it with me now, kids: Grommet. Grommet. Grawwww-met! Grommets are good, because in addition to having an awfully fun name to say, they have all sorts of decorating potential. For those who haven't a clue what I'm babbling about, grommets are basically metal rings that reinforce the holes made in fabric. They're an easy and inexpensive way to create sturdy, finished holes in a wide variety of materials, from light cotton to heavy canvas to plastic tarp (though when you're working with delicate fabrics, you'll want to give your holes additional support by doubling or tripling up the fabric). Turn that ever-versatile bedsheet into a curtain panel with the addition of some grommets; make a no-sew pillow cover by adding grommets along the edges of two squares of fabric, then binding them together with ribbon; add grommets to your dish towels to make them easy to hang on a hook. Inserting grommets is easy; just get yourself a grommet kit, which will include a device for punching holes and attaching grommets, as well as the grommet hardware itself. Grommet kits are available at both hardware stores and fabric stores, though the latter tend to have a bigger selection of sizes and finishes.

to dye for: fabric dye

So you're sick of the boring gray-blue-white color scheme of your current living room, and looking to add a little more fun to your color palette. Before you go on a mad shopping spree for new throw pillows or ditch the old curtains for something in a hipper hue, there's a cool substance you really need to know about: fabric dye. If your fabric's in fine condition and your only quibble with it is its color, you might be able to get away with just giving it a dye job instead of replacing it with something new. Fabric dye comes in a gazillion different colors of the rainbow; you can get formulations that let you dye fabric mess-free in your washer (follow the instructions very, very carefully to ensure that you don't unintentionally color future loads of laundry), or buy hand-dyes if you don't have ready access to your own washing machine.

Armed with the knowledge of these quick-fix tricks, even the biggest decorating slacker has no excuse for making do with drab digs. When you have the right goods in your toolkit, decorating your pad doesn't have to be a chore. So quit procrastinating; ease your lazy decorating self into the do-it-yourself life with these quickie projects—no sewing or carpentry required.

make this: dining chair cover

If you've ever shopped for dining chairs, then you already know: A brand-spanking-new set will cost quite a bit of cash. Even settling for the cheap seats starts to add up once you start buying chairs in the typical multiples of four or six that your dining table probably requires. Fortunately, dining chair bargains are easy to find secondhand. The only catch is that you'll tend to find there's an obvious reason the original owners are pitching their seats—namely, the upholstery will generally be pretty beat.

Never fear, however, as dining chairs are far and away the easiest furnishings you could possibly re-cover. Your typical dining chair will consist of an upholstered cushion on the bottom. And most of the time, this cushion will be removable. With just a screwdriver, a staple gun, and some new fabric, you can give those tired dining chairs a new look in no time flat. First, here's what you'll need:

* Fabric

* Staples

* Staple gun

* Scissors

* Screwdriver

Dining chair with cover

1. Turn your chair upside down and remove the screws that are holding the seat cushion in place. Set the screws aside in a safe place.

2. Measure the seat base you just removed, and add about five inches all around to your measurement. This is the amount of fabric you'll need.

3. Once you have your fabric, place it facedown on the floor. Now center the seat cushion facedown on top of the cloth.

4. Starting with the back edge of the cushion, wrap the fabric up around the edge and over to the wooden seat bottom. Staple the fabric into place along the center and about 1" to 2" in from the edge of the wood.

   Now take the fabric at the front edge of the cushion and firmly wrap it up around the edge and over to the seat bottom. You want to pull the fabric just taut enough to get out the wrinkles, but not so taut that you stretch the fabric all out of shape. Staple the fabric in place along the middle of the front edge, just opposite your first set of staples.

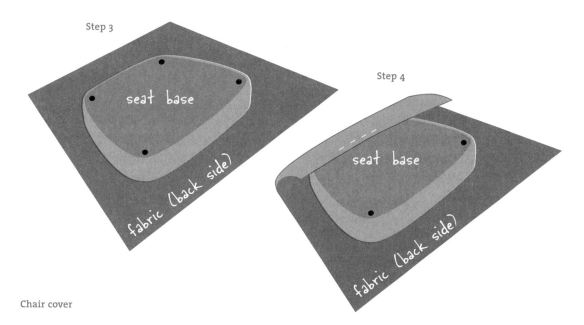

Chair cover

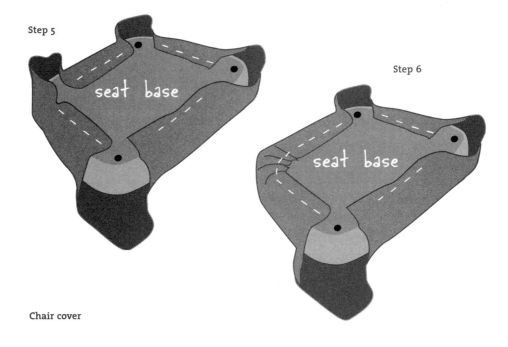

Step 5

seat base

Step 6

seat base

Chair cover

5. Repeat Step 4 with the two remaining sides of the cushion.

6. Time now to deal with those corners. It can take a try or two to get them perfect, so start with the back corners so that any flaws will be less conspicuous. Basically you'll be pulling the fabric taut and distributing the material as evenly as you can in a series of neat pleats. Once you're happy with how the corners look, staple them firmly into place.

7. Trim any excess fabric so that the fabric more or less sits flat against the wood base.

8. Using the screws you saved from Step 1, reattach the cushion to the frame. Now give it a test-drive and have a seat!

make this: fabric roller shades

I've never been a big fan of proper window treatments—drapes and valances and tie-backs and the like. Call me lazy, but it's always seemed like an awful lot of unnecessary fuss over a feature of the home that I generally think looks just fine as is. I like big windows that let in lots of light; even as a kid, I always made sure my curtains were open before I went to

Fabric roller shades

bed at night, so that I'd wake up with the sun hitting my face. Of course, I grew up in the suburbs with a second-story bedroom and sufficient distance between our house and the neighbors; little matters like, oh, privacy, just weren't an issue. But these days, I'm living the city life. And I've had to reconcile myself to the fact that unless I want to be giving the folks in the adjacent apartment building a free peep show every night, window coverings are pretty much a must.

Still, there was no way I could live with the matching faded peach floral curtains and roller blinds that originally came with my pad, no matter how practical those window treatments might be. Down came the curtains, which I promptly stashed out of sight in the darkest deepest depths of my closet. And then it was time to deal with the shade. Fortunately, replacing old, ugly roller shades with whatever fun fabric suits your fancy turns out to be a quickie project that can be easily tackled in a free evening—perfect for slacker decorators. Heck, you don't even need to know how to sew—with the help of some heat-fusible products, you can do it all with an iron and ironing board. Here's what you'll need:

* Fabric—rummage through the remnants bin of your friendly neighborhood fabric store or look for funky vintage tablecloths and curtains at your favorite thrift store for good deals

* Iron-on interfacing (a.k.a. fusible interfacing)

* No-fray liquid (a.k.a. seam sealant)

* No-sew tape (though you can use a sewing machine if you prefer)

* Thread

* Scissors

* Iron and ironing board

* Colored pencil (which will show up on your fabric)

* T-square/straightedge

* Staple gun

* Old roller shade

1. Take down the old roller shade and remove the original material as well as the wooden slat or dowel that weighted it. Scribble a little arrow on the shade barrel to mark which way the fabric fell—this will make your life easier later on when it comes time to reattach. Measure the old material, then add a couple inches to the width and three inches to the length to get your new fabric dimensions. (This assumes that the old shade was already cut to fit your window properly; if you've co-opted an old shade from a different window, you'll basically want the fabric height to be about a foot longer than the height of the window, and the width to be two inches or so more.)

2. Trim your fabric to the proper dimensions and iron the fabric. Make sure you use the heat setting appropriate for your material, unless you want to do what I did on my first attempt at making these shades, which was to meld my polyester fabric to my iron.

3. Read the instructions that came with your interfacing. Trim the interfacing so that it's about the same size as the fabric you cut in the preceding step. Most likely, the directions will inform you to place

Shades: Step 3   Shades: Step 4

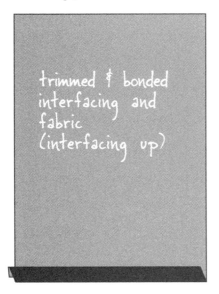

trimmed & bonded
interfacing and
fabric
(interfacing up)

iron

no-sew tape

your fabric wrong-side-up on the ironing board, then line up the interfacing on top, with the adhesive side facing down toward the fabric (the adhesive side will be the rougher side). Working from the center of the fabric, press and glide a steam iron over the interfacing, doing your best to avoid wrinkles. Patience and a gentle touch are key; you'll have to do quite a few passes over the fabric to get the interfacing to stick. Once the interfacing seems more or less bonded, flip the fabric and iron till it's good and flat.

4. Time now to trim the reinforced fabric down to the proper width. Measure the length of the shade barrel; this is how wide you'll want your fabric to be. Use a T-square or straightedge and a colored pencil to mark where you'll cut.

5. Dab the no-fray liquid all along both penciled lines. Let dry, then carefully trim your fabric using scissors. Cut in long, smooth strokes to keep your edges as neat as possible.

6. After trimming, you might discover that your interfacing isn't quite stuck to the edges in a few spots. Iron all along the edges until well

sealed; you can also use just a bit of no-fray to give the edges more help in the bonding department.

7. Fold the bottom edge of the fabric to make a ¾" hem. Then make another fold that's a little bigger than the height of the wooden slat or dowel you reserved in Step 1. Cut a piece of no-sew tape that will stretch the width of the fabric, then tuck the tape between the shade and the doubled-over fold. Iron (again, use the appropriate heat setting for your material) until you have a nice, secure hem. Slide in the wooden slat/dowel.

8. Use a staple gun to attach the top edge of your new shade to the shade barrel, making certain that the shade falls in the right direction.

Roll it up, install, and enjoy!

chapter twelve

fight the chaos

Sometime during the college years, I acquired the reputation for being a chaos magnet. I, of course, always liked to blame the mess on the endless cycle of art projects that I was perpetually in various stages of completing—neatness hampers creativity, right? When that excuse failed me, there was always my takeout-loving, dining hall tray–accumulating roommate who (much as I adored her as a friend) could go a lot longer than I could before escorting those half-eaten plates of dining hall spaghetti mush back from whence they came.

Then I moved into a place of my own. And after many years of denying the truth, I'm 'fessing up. There's just no getting around the evidence: I'm a messy person by nature.

I just can't seem to do anything without leaving major physical evidence of the activity. I collect stuff, and I generate stuff: If there's a smallest spare nook in the house, I'll use it to pile ever more stuff. All this mess would be fine if I felt comfortable with the chaos. If I didn't mind excavating a mountain of shoes thrown carelessly in my closet in order to find that perfect pair of black boots, or if I didn't loathe the sight of a living room teeming with mounds of old magazines and new books—if I felt at home living in a certifiable disaster area, my inherent untidiness wouldn't be a problem. But I'm the worst sort of messy person, you see, because I can't stand my own slobbish tendencies. Really, what I need is a maid. Sadly, financial reality continues to put a damper on those dreams.

So believe me when I tell you: I understand how hard it is to keep a neat home. Housework is a chore; organization is tedious. But what's the point of spending all that time hunting down the perfect lamp, fixing up that yard sale sofa, and tweaking your furniture arrangement until it's exactly right if you're just going to camouflage all your decorating efforts in clutter? A little bit of apartment maintenance here and there goes a long way toward making a home not just livable, but lovable, too.

cull, baby, cull

The first step (and alas, I'm afraid there's no getting around this) is to conquer those pack-rat tendencies and learn to cull. Take inventory of your belongings and decide whether each object you've accumulated is something you use often, something you use occasionally, something of sentimental value, or just plain junk. The first you'll need out and about, the second and third can go into storage, and the fourth should either be jettisoned or recycled (donate it to charity, have a yard sale, give it to a friend—get rid of it). Be ruthless. You don't need your notes from freshman year psych. Really.

If you're a die-hard pack rat, you're probably plugging your ears with your fingers and singing "tra-la-la" right now. The mere mention of the word "cull" gets your heart racing in fear as your mind starts spinning out rationalizations as an automatic defense mechanism to protect your precious voluminous stuff.

But quit worrying. Really. I'm not going to tell you to pitch your collection of vintage cookbooks or Wolverine action figures because, hey, I'm not going to part with mine, either. The weird little things that no one but you loves are exactly what make your space distinctly, wonderfully yours—and if they take up space, so be it. In my own stuff-packed home, I figure that's space well spent, even if it means my pad never quite looks as pristinely perfect as the minimalist pads I drool over in decorating magazines.

But let's face it: There's the good kind of useless stuff, the stuff that

makes us smile and bask in the glow of nostalgia, and then there's the kind that serves no other function than to take up space. The sort of stuff that's just there because we've forgotten it exists (as it turned out to be useless), or because it was a present (that we didn't like), or because we're just plain incapable of making a decision regarding what else to do with it, now that it's just junk. And the longer you put off doing something about it, the more junk you'll have, until one day in the not-too-distant future, you're one of those scary people who has to dig out a path to the door each morning because your pad is overflowing with mountains of stuff that you can't

a plan for weeding

Visualize a new use for the soon-to-be-empty space. Keep your goal in mind while you are clearing away the junk. Put this newly uncluttered space to good use or you may be tempted to fill it with more of the same junk!

Have plenty of containers ready to carry the materials away. You don't want to run out of them in the middle of your cleaning, potentially leaving the remainder of the junk pile to linger for months or (gasp!) years. Organize the following:

File folders. For any papers that need to be put away, bills that need to be paid, Post-it notes that need attending to.

Storage box(es). For the stuff you use seasonally or when the odd whim strikes; this stuff can go in the back of a cabinet, on a shelf in the closet, in a plastic storage container that you slide under your sofa—anywhere not too challenging to get to.

Deep storage box(es). For the stuff you're hanging on to for a very good reason, but don't need ready access to; this is the stuff you store in the basement, in the attic, in the garage—all those out-of-the-way storage places.

Donate/sell box(es). For the stuff that you don't personally need but that someone else might.

even remember acquiring in the first place. Don't be that person: Get a handle on the junk now.

In theory, culling should be easy. You toss the useless, the broken, the dated, the hopelessly hideous, and keep the rest. You make this a seasonal process if you're really on top of things, a yearly one more likely; at the very least, you perform the process each time you make the move to a new set of digs. But if weeding is such a cinch, why are so many of us still cramming our closets full to the point where opening them becomes a genuine safety hazard?

Trash bags/recycle bin. For the stuff that no one else could conceivably want, either.

Big fat marker. To label your boxes, lest you inadvertently give away those family heirlooms that were supposed to be bound for the back of your closet.

Set aside a short period of time to weed the junk. For example, give yourself only fifteen minutes to gather those magazines into bags or recycling bins. The short amount of time guarantees that you will not dawdle and leaf through each issue to look for an interesting article that will cause you to keep the magazine (and all the ones like it). Working under a self-imposed deadline will give you only enough time to collect the materials and head for the door.

Ask a non–pack-rat friend to help you. Choose someone who you know won't let you keep anything you don't absolutely need.

Have the getaway car ready. If you are donating items to Goodwill or another local charity, be sure you can move the items straight from your place to the car and off to their final destination all in the same day. Otherwise, that large box of well-intentioned donations might stay in the hallway forever.

Like most aspects of keeping house, weeding sounds scary when you think about applying it to your whole house. Taking inventory of the entirety of your twenty-some years of accumulated stuff? Way too intimidating. Which is why we're going to make it a wee bit easier for all you pack rats and guide you through the process one little room at a time.

the living room

There's a definite and direct correlation between the amount of clutter in a room and the time in which we actually spend in it. This, then, explains the living room.

Our living rooms are the rooms in which we curl up each night to read books, watch movies, even eat meals. It's where we'll sit to open mail or bang away on our laptops, make a birthday card for someone special, or mend a hole in a sweater. Gone unchecked, our coffee tables have a tendency to accumulate books and magazines, clothes to be fixed and laundry to be folded, to the point where it becomes a major feat just to find space to set down a mug of tea. With all the living that goes on in this room, it's no wonder that the living room tends to be the room that's in direst need of a good culling.

Start with the no-brainer stuff first: If you have any clothing strewn anywhere in the living room, find another home for it. Coats and other outerwear go in a closet or coatrack; all other clothing belongs in the bedroom if it's clean or in a hamper if it's not. Seriously, I know this might sound obvious, but I know all too well how easy it is to let the coats pile up on that unused armchair, to let the folded (maybe) laundry sit on the edge of the coffee table while you wait for that elusive free moment to get around to putting it away. Quit making excuses and deal with it now. In all likelihood, your abode is small enough that it will take just a millisecond more—tops—to dig your jacket out of the closet or off a wall hook than it would to grab it from the back of the sofa when you want to go out.

With your clothing picked up and stowed away in its proper place (congratulations!), you should now be able to see your sofa. Next up is the coffee table. If your pad is anything like mine, the coffee table has a tendency to get covered by newspapers waiting to be recycled and magazines waiting to be read. Unless you're living in a dentist's waiting room, however, there is no reason to have more than one newspaper and a couple of magazines out on the table at any given time. Any newspaper other than the one from today should go directly in your recycling box; you're not maintaining an archive here. Magazines are a little trickier to deal with, as you might find yourself flipping through that issue of *Budget Living* from three months ago and realize there's a project in there you'd really like to try. Here's where you just have to be honest with yourself—are you ever *really* going to put the ideas in that fabulous article to use? Really and truly? Seriously? If after a good ponder you can firmly answer yes, snip out that article and start a binder for this and other clippings. The rest of the magazine can go into the recycling bin. If you have any whole magazines for which you have no use, you might also consider donating those to a thrift shop or finding out if a used bookstore wants them.

With your surfaces cleared and tidied, it's time to turn to your bookshelves, entertainment center, and other open nooks. Look through your books, CDs, DVDs, and videotapes, and pull out anything that you can safely say you have no interest in ever reading through, listening to, or watching ever again. That book on the making of the atomic bomb from some college history course, the one you never bothered to read even back when it might have behooved you to do so, that En Vogue CD you won at your middle school raffle—these are not items that are making your life better in any way, shape, or form. So stop hanging on to them—into the donate/sell box they go. The best part is that you can bring these goods to a used bookstore or record store; while it's likely that you won't be able to sell everything you cart in, you'll probably be able to get some trade-in or cash for at least a portion of it—providing you with an opportunity to buy new books, music, and movies that you might actually enjoy.

There's only one more thing to deal with: knickknacks. Before your inner pack rat starts hyperventilating at the mere thought that I'm going to tell you to purge your treasured Buffy collectibles, relax: I'm a lover of myriad useless objects myself, and I'm not going to make you depersonalize your nest just for the sake of a slightly more streamlined room. I am, however, going to suggest you give all that stuff a serious assessment. Do you really love all the cow-print paraphernalia dotting your bookshelves, or was it just something you sort of liked way back when you were thirteen, that your family continues to insist is "your thing" by supplementing your collection at every gift-giving opportunity? Do you really need fifty sno globes gathering dust on your entertainment center, or could you pick out ten of your very favorites to make the same kitschy cool statement, rotating new ones in whenever you get bored? Why have a tiki mug strewn in every corner of the room when you could consolidate them into a single location for maximum tiki impact and a less haphazard look? If each and every one of those nonutilitarian doodads is there because you genuinely can't bear not to gaze upon them on a daily basis, that's fine: They serve a function, even if that function is only apparent to you. But if there's anything that you're not deeply attached to, it's probably just taking up space that could be better used to highlight other goodies that you love a whole lot more.

After a weekend morning spent sorting and shuffling and purging, you'll find yourself with cleared-off coffee tables you can actually set a cup of coffee upon, shelves that can actually accommodate those finds you bring back from your next thrift store excursion, end tables where you can set a remote control without worrying it'll get consumed by the chaos— yes, a living room you can actually *live* in.

the kitchen

Maybe this has happened to you. One fine morning, following your usual breakfast routine, you open a cabinet to grab a box of cereal—and find yourself rudely awakened by an avalanche of hot cocoa mix and tea, granola and crackers and pudding mix that comes a-tumbling atop your sleepy head. Or you find that your foodstuffs have usurped your countertops, and you've been vanquished to the kitchen table to do your slicing and dicing. Whether you need more space for cooking up a storm or for storing your myriad preprepped eats, it's time to take control of your kitchen.

Start with the cabinets and drawers first, as you'll need to maximize that storage space in order to deal with the rest of the kitchen chaos. Working one cabinet or drawer at a time, empty out the space and assess the contents. Examine each item, and make a firm decision about whether it will be kept in the kitchen, put into regular or deep storage, donated to a worthy cause, or hurled in the trash.

Dump any food products that have an expired date, that haven't seen the light of day since your last weeding session, or that are supporting another form of life. Chuck that box of nasty candy your great aunt gave you last Christmas, the ones you have no intention of ever ingesting. That collection of freebie plastic cups from the 7-Eleven, the ones that are barely a step above disposable-grade plastic? Pitch them into the trash bag (or recycling, if possible).

The definite kitchen keepers are also pretty easy to pick out. Any item you use in cooking or otherwise eat at least once a month should obviously stay put, as should any of the edibles that you're genuinely planning to consume. But if you last used that garlic press a year ago, is that sufficient grounds for keeping it in the kitchen arsenal? A few things to consider:

1. Are you really planning to use this tool again?

2. If that someday is in a future date far, far away, will it genuinely make your kitchen work faster/simpler/better, and will it be too expensive to just go buy yourself another one?

If the answer to number one is really a no, question yourself no further. That apple corer, the egg slicer, the salad spinner that gave you a callus on that one occasion when you tried to use it? If the objects in question aren't ones that are actually of use to you personally, say buh-bye, and place the object in your donate/sell box. If the answer to question one is a maybe, then hang onto the doodad only if its price would make it impossible for you ever to get your hands on a replacement, should the occasion arise where having the tool or appliance handy would genuinely make your life easier. Put it in regular storage if you think you'll use it maybe once a year, deep storage if less often.

Of course, there's still all that stuff that we manage to accumulate that's useful but not essential. Those promo bike bottles you've snagged through your yearly Walk for Hunger, Run for Breast Cancer, Skip for Whatever? Sure, you've been known to bring them on hikes and picnics. But unless there's a really compelling reason why you need to have a different one for every day of the week, pick out one or two of your favorites, and place the rest in the donate box. The same goes for multiple sets of silverware and extra pots and pans. The one possible exception is glassware—if you're a klutz like me, you probably break glasses on a semiregular basis, which makes it a good idea to hang onto as much as space permits. If your cabinets are really jam-packed, either pack up your extra glassware and put it into deep storage, or install open shelving or stemware racks to accommodate them.

Anything that has true-blue sentimental value should be saved and put into deep storage. The twelve-person place setting of fine china that you inherited from your grandmother, now that's something you might want to have around someday, even if you're currently residing in a 375-square-foot studio that can accommodate three guests maximum. Find a place to tuck away these sorts of items for safekeeping—in the closet, under the bed, in the garage, in your parents' basement, at your honey's apartment, wherever.

With your cabinets and drawers carefully weeded, it's time to take a good hard look at what's floating around on the countertops and around your major appliances. If at all possible, store any small appliances that you don't use on a regular basis. Stuff like the food processor, the juicer, and the Crock-Pot can be put away when they're not in use; you'll find yourself with a whole lot more workspace on your counters. In the area around your sink, consolidate your scrubbing tools—toss any that you never use, are so worn out that they're losing integrity, or leave a lingering odor on your hands after you touch them. You should never really need more than one sponge, one dishrag, one scouring pad, and maybe a scrub brush.

Finally, get your fridge décor under control. I'm all for the personality-packed, picture-dense fridge, but don't just slap up your snaps haphazardly. Just because your best friend from college sent it to you doesn't mean you have to tack it up. Keep your favorites up on the fridge and put the rest away in your photo albums. I like to organize mine into a collage to keep them looking neat. As for any notes, coupons, and papers that you've stuck on your fridge, keep them localized to one area—I use the side of the fridge rather than the front so they're less visible—and toss them out when you no longer need them. Clip magnets are great for keeping those take-out menus neatly confined on the fridge—although if you can find drawer space for them, you get extra props.

With your kitchen streamlined, give yourself a big pat on the back and take some time to enjoy all that freed-up cooking space.

the bathroom

Generally speaking, the bathroom is far and away the tiniest room in the house. This is why it never ceases to amaze me how much stuff I can still manage to squeeze into it. I used to blame it on inadequate storage—until I moved from a place with a good-sized bathroom, complete with fabulous double sinks and ample cabinetry, into a pad featuring a tiny closet-of-a-bathroom that offered no stash space whatsoever. Living with a miniscule bathroom forced me to take a long, hard look at the things I was keeping in my bath space—and what I discovered was that most of it didn't really need to be in the bathroom at all.

On your next lazy Sunday afternoon, pull out all the potions and lotions and other junk that's no doubt spilling out from your bathroom. Take a good look at what you have, and toss out anything that gets so little use that you'd completely forgotten about its existence. That tube of lipstick you've had since you were seventeen, the stick of deodorant that made you break out in hives, that collection of travel-sized toiletries filched from hotels; trust me, if you haven't used them in the last year, you're never going to use them.

Stash stuff out of sight whenever possible. There is no reason in the world why you need to display your entire toiletry collection in the space around your sink. Anything you don't use on a daily basis should be stowed away—in the medicine cabinet, in a drawer, on a shelf, even in another room if necessary. The same thing goes for the twenty bottles of shampoos, conditioners, bubble baths, exfoliating scrubs, and the like that stand like sentinels around the edge of your tub. Any that don't get regular use—at least once weekly—should either be tossed (if you never use them) or put away (if you use them every once in a while). And if you have multiple half-empty bottles of any of your favorite toiletries, combine them and pitch the extra empty containers to free up space.

With your toiletries culled and tidied, it's time to address the subject of bathroom reading. If you're a big believer in making good use of your commode time to catch up on light reading, fine. As a great lover of words, I'm all for squeezing in the reading whenever you can. But you do not need to maintain a complete library in the tiny confines of your bathroom. Any magazines or newspapers that you have pored over from end to end should be sent to the recycling bin. As for books, rotate your reading and restrict yourself to one or two tomes in the bathroom at a time. In addition to the fact that keeping piles of books in the bathroom takes up space that's probably in short supply to begin with, the damp, mold-friendly, toilet-overflow-prone bathroom environment is not a terribly hospitable one for your beloved books.

the bedroom

Bedrooms are private spaces, which explains why it's so easy for them to degenerate into great pits of despair. After all, the threat of other folks actually discovering our filthy habits provides one of the greatest incentives for cleaning sprees. Your living room, the kitchen, the bathroom—these are the public rooms, the ones we'll usually take the time to render presentable whenever we know that folks will be coming over. If anything, the bedroom is where we throw all the junk from the rest of the house; when guests are due to arrive in an hour or less and you have a mountain of stuff that has no obvious home, you can always shove it in the bedroom and close the door. Out of sight, out of mind—until it comes time for you to call it a night, and you realize that between the house junk and the towering heaps of sweaters and shirts, you can't find your bed.

Instead of creating ever more mounds on your dresser, your night table, the foot of your bed, or the floor, take your next free Sunday to weed through the clutter. In the bedroom, the chaos is probably attributable to one main source: clothing. Unless you're lucky enough to have scored a walk-in closet in your apartment, there's probably a limited amount of storage space available for your wardrobe. And if your closets and drawers are already packed so full that you can barely open them, it's no wonder you can't go to the bother of putting away your laundry. But when was the last time you took a really good look at what clothing was actually lurking in the deepest darkest recesses of your dresser?

Take your next free Sunday to pull out each and every item in your wardrobe and assess what you have. Pull out anything you haven't worn in over a year; unless the item in question is of exceptionally high quality, like potentially a collectible once it gets sufficiently old, there is no point keeping that out-of-date bit of clothing around on the off-chance it'll come back into style in ten years. Those jeans that no longer seem cut right, that

no sweat!

Every year, no matter how vigilant I am about dry cleaning and storage, winter rolls around and I discover that I've lost a few more of my favorite sweaters to the insects. I'll go to put on a beloved soft blue sweater, only to discover that there's a big section that has more holes than a hunk of Swiss cheese. In the past, I'd sigh and toss the sweater into my Goodwill pile. That is, until I realized I could recycle these babies and use them for exciting, new purposes.

One of the best ways to put those old sweaters to good use is by felting them. Take any of your holey 100 percent wool sweaters (no blends). Now get wacky and ignore that little label telling to you dry clean only. Toss your wool sweaters in the washing machine, launder (hot water for light colors; cool water for brights), then tumble dry. What emerges is a nice dense material that won't unravel (too badly) when cut; snip away the bug-nibbled bits and you're ready to start playing. Sew together felted wool pieces to make throw pillow covers, cut them into squares and make a quilt, or use the material in whatever other fabric project you like. Get crafty!

sweater that's riddled with moth holes, those way-cool shoes that you never wear because they make you feel like you're walking on nails—into the donate/sell box they go.

Now separate the remaining items into in-season clothes and out-of-season clothes. Put the latter into storage, and return the former to either the closet or a drawer. Rotating your wardrobe according to the seasons will not only free up heaps of closet face, but by forcing yourself to do the twice yearly winter-to-summer, summer-to-winter clothing switch, you'll be far more likely to purge those outdated, ill-fitting, and moth-nibbled clothes on a regular basis.

You should now find you have plenty of additional space, which means it's time to finally put away those stacks of clean laundry. Fold 'em up, hang 'em up, tuck 'em out of sight. As for dirty laundry, anything washable goes into the hamper—yes, you really do need one—and the dry cleanables go into a bag, which you should put by the front door so you'll remember to actually take it with you next time you go out.

With all that clothing picked up and put away in its proper place, you should finally be able to see your bed again. Reward yourself for all that hard work; flop down, curl up, and take a well-deserved nap.

the office

Whether it consists of a single desk in the corner of your living room, a dedicated spot of counter by the entrance to your kitchen or even an actual room, your home office is the place where paper tends to congregate. It's amazing that something so thin can create so much mess. Those bills you have yet to deal with, the random Post-it notes you've scribbled to your roommate, your sweetie, yourself, whomever—taken on an individual basis, they don't take up much space. But what starts off as a neat little pile of the day's mail soon breeds and multiplies. The lazy person way of dealing with this generally involves sliding the old paper stuff over and stacking the new paper stuff on top, until your office space looks like one big, solid mass of paper.

Instead of creating ever larger and more precariously balanced piles, take the time to confront that junk that's covering your desk. Separate your stuff into three piles: stuff that needs to be dealt with, stuff that needs to be saved, and stuff that serves no function whatsoever. Huck everything in the last category into the recycling or trash can, then start filing away all items that fit into the second category. With any luck, you should now have enough space on your desk to look over the remaining stuff—stuff that requires your immediate attention, like your credit card bills and loan payments, that article you need to review for work, or the birthday card you have to send out to your mom by Friday. Pull out your checkbook, a pen, and whatever else you might need. Now put that newly cleared desk space to good use.

after-school special: culling school stuff

School is out—and for good! So why are you still hanging on to all those old notes? Yes, there's a special category of junk that most of us find ourselves hoarding in the recent postcollege years. In the mad rush to clear out of your dorm room after graduation, you probably threw all your school stuff into a couple of boxes, slapped on the packing tape, and forgot about it. Lurking in the back of your hall closet, the trunk of your car, or in your parents' basement, those boxes still sit unopened. Free up that space and sort through your college junk now. Here's a guide to what to keep and what to pitch.

Item	Shelf Life	Reason to Keep or Toss
School Stuff		
Textbooks	Forever	Your professional library should reflect what you studied in school. Keep all the books you spared from the book buy-back scam that textbook stores run at the end of each semester.

Item	Shelf Life	Reason to Keep or Toss
School Stuff (continued)		
Class notes	Three months	Unless you are continuing on to a related graduate or postgraduate program, your notes will only be taking up space. Yes, they were helpful in the past, but what is the likelihood that you will read through your notes after you graduate? Let's be honest, now.
Tests	Three months	Along with notes, the usefulness of tests (the actual paper copies) expire soon after school ends. If you are continuing in a career that relates to your degree, it is every employer's hope that you have synthesized the content of those tests. Keep them around if you continue on in an advanced degree program.
Course packs	Six months	If you have some absolutely relevant articles that you can use for work or continuing education purpose, keep the course packs for a year. If the three-inch-thick flimsy tomes are bending under their own weight and making your otherwise stellar book collection look sloppy, jot down the title, author, and publication data of your favorite articles, and toss the pack. Unless they are unpublished papers, you will be able to retrieve the article from a university library.
Periodicals, journals, magazines	Six months	Like course packs, periodicals and journals will outlive their usefulness in bulk. Pare down your collection as much as you can, and save the articles that most impact your professional career.

Item	Shelf Life	Reason to Keep or Toss
School Stuff (continued)		
Term papers	Forever	In addition to being tangible products of your scholarly labor, term papers are a handy resource if you ever need to send in a writing sample for a job.
Documents		
Grade reports	Three months	Keep these only long enough to compare them to your official transcript. Make sure that what you received each semester is correctly reflected on the transcript. If, however, you received written evaluations instead of letter grades (some programs do this), keep the evaluations to show employers.
Original transcripts	Forever	Your original transcript will most likely arrive with your diploma in the mail. You can always request copies from your school's administration office, but it's a good idea to keep the original one in a safe place.
Diploma	Forever	No matter how you display it, you should keep the sheepskin.
Bills		
Tuition bill	Forever	Keep these to torment your future children: "When I was your age, tuition was only $25,000 a year!"
All other school bills	One day	Burn upon payment.

stow away!

Unless you live like a monk, even whittling down the junk will still leave you with a fair amount of stuff. Having survived the culling process, it's time to tackle the task of finding homes for all your remaining goods.

While finding spots to squirrel away your stuff is obviously more challenging in some pads than in others, even the puniest of city studio apartments offers plenty of storage potential. Your storage areas can be crammed to the gills, as long as you're smart about how you pack them. A little organization can work wonders to ensure that all that stuff is sensibly stowed—out of the way when you don't need it, readily accessible whenever you do. Here are a few tips for eking out every last bit of stash space from your apartment.

into the closet

Sure, it's a lot easier to just haphazardly jam all the junk you don't want to look at into a closet, quickly containing the chaos with a hip check to the door before the contents tumble down from their perches. Of course, the next time you open that closet door, you're guaranteed to encounter an avalanche—which means that not only will you have used that precious closet space inefficiently, but you'll have to waste additional time trying to stuff everything back in. A little forethought *will* allow you to cram even more goods into existing closets and cabinets, and avoid a concussion to boot. Items that you use more often should be easier to get to than items that you only need access to occasionally. Your cooking pots should go at the front of the cabinet, while the fondue pot can be shoved farther into the back; the vacuum cleaner shouldn't be stuffed behind a mountain of sports equipment, unless you're *really* trying to avoid cleaning your abode.

Hammer some nails—or even better, install proper hooks—on the sides of the closet and the backside of the door. Invest in a few of those gigantic plastic storage containers, then stack them up neatly inside, making sure, of course, to put the stuff you'll need access to at the top. Get hanging

shelf bags for shoes, or use a shoe rack. Alternatively, consider getting yourself one of those metal wire shelf kits. The kits come with an assortment of poles and shelves that let you compartmentalize your space however you see fit. Head over to your nearest home goods megastore, where you'll find more organizing options than you could possibly have imagined existed.

think vertical

When we think about how much space we have in our digs, we tend to be so focused on the square footage—or lack thereof—that it's easy to forget about that great big area lurking above the floor. Even if your pad is crammed with furniture, you're likely to have free space above the sofa, next to the entryway, above the kitchen counters, or in the top of some closet. These spots are just screaming for a wall shelf (or two, or three).

In addition to adding wall shelving, you can also maximize your vertical space usage by adjusting the shelving in your existing cabinets and bookcases. Many of these storage units come with predrilled holes on the inside edges that allow you to shift your shelves up and down easily by simply moving the pegs that serve as support. Some of the cabinets in my kitchen originally had only one shelf dividing each into two compartments; to accommodate more of our glassware, we lowered the height of the existing shelf and added a new one on top. Voila—50 percent more storage in the cabinet, without taking up any additional space in the kitchen itself.

by the book

Bookshelves can be particularly challenging to use efficiently, as books have a pesky tendency to come in a wide assortment of sizes and shapes. Here's a hint: Stack books on their backs as well as their spines. "Blasphemy!" you book lovers out there may be shouting right now—how can you pull your dog-eared copy of *Catcher in the Rye* off the shelf to read if it's pinned beneath a dozen other books? But hear me out. Stacking books on top of one another is far and away the most efficient use of the vertical space between shelves. Obviously, any books to which you require ready and instant access should be stored standing upright. But let's face it, a good portion of your collection has probably been sitting on your shelves for years and years now, collecting dust. These are the books that can be stacked on top of one another. Organize these books into piles according to size and dimension. Pocket-size paperbacks, trade paperbacks, hardcover novels, college textbooks—each of these should go in a separate pile. Now slide your stacks onto your bookshelves. You'll generally find that alternating a horizontal stack with a series of vertically standing books yields the most attractive results.

what lurks beneath

Besides wall space, most apartments offer plenty of little nooks and crannies that make for perfect storage areas. Under the bed, under the sofa, under your desk—those areas beneath your furniture offer prime stash-it potential that frequently goes unused. Mosey over to your favorite cheapo department store and procure a few of those long, flat plastic storage containers; stuff them full, then slide them out of sight under your couch or bed. While you're at it, pick up some wicker storage baskets or leather cubes, and use them to hide stored stuff under the coffee table. Get resourceful and put all those "under" spaces to good use.

Don't forget about the "behind" spaces either. Behind the dresser, behind the bookshelf, behind the wardrobe—all of these spots offer perfect storage for flat goods. They're especially handy for stashing extra moving boxes. Just break apart and flatten all those empty boxes you can't bear to part with; you'll be amazed how many boxes you can now cram into just a few inches of space.

multitasking it

Choose furniture that also offers storage space. Tables that have drawers, for instance, are infinitely more practical than those that don't. But don't be afraid to think outside the box a little, either. A table doesn't have to be a slab of wood with four legs holding it up by the corners. Need an office desk? Buy a solid wooden door at your favorite home improvement store, paint it in whatever color makes you happy, then throw it on a couple of file cabinets—instant desk with plenty of room to store all your papers. Instead of a traditional coffee table, use a low bookshelf (put it on casters for mobility) or a trunk (yard sales and estate sales are great places to score some nice vintage trunks). Get creative and make your furnishings serve double duty to maximize your storage potential.

With all your stuff culled, tidied, and stashed away in its proper place, you're ready to get down to the nitty-gritty of home maintenance. Yes, folks, it's time to talk about cleaning.

clean as a whistle

A college friend of mine once proclaimed with defensive pride, "I'm messy, but not dirty!" It's an important distinction: While the former trait merely makes it difficult for one to find what one's looking for at any given moment, the latter trait has many more potentially unpleasant consequences—grimy furnishings, rancid odors, nasty germs, and more fun perks to ensure that your digs won't be fit for human inhabitation. Sure, for most of us, cleaning house is a drag, but with the right equipment and a sensible array of handy household cleaning products, the job becomes a whole lot easier. Time to stock up.

the cleaning arsenal

Keep these cleaning tools on hand:

Rags. Some people like to use sponges to work away at dirt and grime, but personally, I find that recycling old socks and T-shirts for rags works fabulously.

Lint-free cloths. Essential for dusting and cleaning glass. There's absolutely no point in trying to get rid of dust with a regular cloth, since it'll only leave a trail of lint behind every time you wipe.

Hand-held scrub brush. For scrubbing bathtubs, floors, and other medium-large surfaces.

Small scrub brush. For getting those pesky grout lines clean, as well as cleaning in tight areas around fixtures; an old toothbrush works really well for this purpose.

Toilet brush. Yes, it's an icky job, but that toilet must be cleaned, and you'll need this tool to do it properly.

Mop. For cleaning the kitchen floor and other hard flooring.

Plastic bucket with handle. For use with your mop.

Dustpan and brush. For cleaning up small messes.

Vacuum cleaner. Yes, I'll admit it; I went for way too long relying on a broom to clean house for the sole reason that I was too damn cheap to get myself a vacuum cleaner. So I know how easy it is to justify not rushing out to buy a vacuum as soon as you move into your first very own digs—those suckers (bad pun, I know) don't come cheap. If you can afford it at all, though, a nice, powerful, new vacuum cleaner is a very smart investment. It'll last you for years and get your abode a gazillion times cleaner than any old broom ever could. If budget concerns are really, truly an issue, hunt down an old vacuum cleaner at a garage sale or borrow an old one from parents or other relatives.

the basic cleaning agents

A trip to your supermarket's cleaning aisle will reveal that there's a specific cleaning product for just about every single item in your house. You could stock a dozen different cleansers if you wanted to, but it's also possible to clean house with just a few simple products.

Baking soda. There is no reason in the world that you should not have baking soda in your house right now. In addition to being a cooking essential, it also has many other potential household uses. For one thing, it's a great mild abrasive cleanser—just mix a little baking soda with enough water to form a paste, and you have a great scrub to use to clean your stovetop, kitchen counters, bathroom sink, whatever. (You can also do it the lazy way, by sprinkling soda directly on the surface, then attacking it with a damp rag.) Baking soda also has a handy odor-absorbing capability—pop an open container into your fridge to keep it smelling nice and fresh, or wherever you need to combat nasty odors.

Vinegar/lemon juice. Thanks to their acidic properties, vinegar and lemon juice are both excellent for getting rid of alkaline hard water stains and buildup (lime and other mineral deposits will soften if you let them sit in a little vinegar or lemon juice for an hour or so), as well as cutting through greasy, oily residue. Lemon juice is milder and easier on the nose; vinegar has a bit more punch.

Glass cleaner = one part vinegar to two parts water. If you're getting streaks with this solution, try adding a smidgen of liquid soap or detergent to cut through any waxy residue that might be on your glass surface.

Grease cutter = one part lemon juice or vinegar to one part water.

Wood polish = one part lemon juice to two parts vegetable oil.

Antibacterial/mold/mildew agent. Pour straight white vinegar in a spray bottle and apply directly where needed. Yeah, it stinks, but the smell *will* dissipate after a few hours.

Liquid soap/detergent. Essential for cutting through grease and oil, liquid soaps or detergent loosen soil so that you can easily wipe it away; a splash of detergent mixed with water is often all you need to get things clean.

A note about antibacterial products: It seems like every cleaning agent out there now is of the antibacterial variety, which, personally, I find rather vexing. It's best to wade through the labels and find a normal soap if you can, since antibacterial soaps have a tendency to kill off the weak bacteria, encouraging super-strong unstoppable bacteria to flourish in its wake.

the heavy hitters

While natural products are certainly better for the environment, relying solely on baking soda and vinegar to deal with all your household cleaning needs requires an awful lot of elbow grease (added to which, vinegar's kind of malodorous; there's really no getting around that). Having a few choice heavier-duty chemical agents on hand will make it a lot easier for you to deal with tough stains and stubborn grime.

Multipurpose/all-purpose liquid cleaner. For cleaning large surfaces, namely floors and walls, it's a good idea to keep a bottle of liquid all-purpose cleaner on hand. They generally come in concentrate form, with directions printed on the bottle to tell you how to dilute for various household uses.

Multisurface spray cleaner. You could buy a separate tub-and-tile cleaner and glass cleaner, but personally, I like to keep things simple by stocking the bare number of bottles necessary in my cleaning cabinet. Multisurface cleaners work for ceramic, porcelain, chrome, glass, and more.

Barkeeper's Friend. Barkeeper's Friend is a mild abrasive powder that gets your pots, pans, and other metal appliances looking shiny and pretty and new, without scratching up the surface. This is my new favorite cleaning product, and an absolute must have if you have any stainless steel products or appliances in your abode.

Oil soap spray. For keeping a beautiful sheen on your good wood furniture, invest in some oil soap spray (Murphy's is the most common brand). It keeps your wood clean and dust-free without drying it out.

With your cleaning cabinet sensibly stocked, you're ready to clean house. Roll up your sleeves, throw on your favorite loud music, and get working.

keeping the clutter away

So you've tossed out the useless crap? Found the perfect place to stash away all the rest? Stockpiled all the critical cleaning equipment, tools, and products that you'll need to render your digs spic and span? Great, you've taken some important steps toward gaining control of your mess.

But don't breathe too big a sigh of relief, because sadly, the housekeeping duties will keep on coming. The most important thing now is to continue the clutter-and-cleaning patrol. Keep tossing the junk as it finds its way into your now tidy nest, repeating the culling process from time to time; when you take something out of storage, be good about returning it to its proper home after you're done using it. You'll find that a little anal-retentiveness on the organization front really does pay off, because as long as you tidy up before the chaos spins too wildly out of control, cleaning house really shouldn't take all that much time.

Unless you're a neat freak by nature, a little training may be necessary to get yourself into good apartment-maintenance habits. Consider creating a cleaning ritual for yourself. Reserve the night before your recycling bin gets picked up for sifting through newspapers, magazines, mail, and other paper stuff; make Saturday laundry day and Sunday cleaning day. Too busy on weekends? Divide your housekeeping duties by room and schedule half-hour cleaning sprees throughout the week. Save Monday nights for the living room, Tuesdays for the bathroom, Wednesdays for the bedroom, Thursdays for laundry, and get into the habit of tidying the kitchen after each meal. Squeeze your cleaning into short bursts during the workweek and come the weekend, you can kick back, relax, and play.

However you divvy up the tasks throughout your week, stick to the plan. Skip just a cleaning session or two, and you'll rapidly discover that dirt and clutter have a way of multiplying exponentially, in a frighteningly short period of time. If despite your best efforts, you discover that your freewheeling self just can't deal with such a strictly scheduled life, at least keep a household to-do list. Add tasks as you think of them, keeping the list posted prominently in your pad. And get yourself a chalkboard or dry erase board for the list making—so you don't create more housework for yourself by leaving endless piles of Post-it to-dos.

Whether you're implementing a housework schedule or opting for the less rigid to-do list route, be vigilant and tackle messes before they get out of hand. Because disorder is always lurking around the corner. Clean up a little at a time, but often, and you can easily keep the chaos at bay.

keep diggin' it

**m**aybe you've reached these final pages of *First Digs* and are looking around in dismay at your ratty hand-me-down sofa and beat-up rental carpeting. You have a long way to go, you think, before you're living in the sort of digs that anyone would ever feature in a home-decorating book.

Quit beating yourself up and remember this: Ideals are a great thing to aim for, but ultimately, great digs aren't about perfection. My favorite pads aren't necessarily the ones in which every piece of furniture looks like a work of art, and every object is placed just so. Frankly, I don't have a lot of interest in houses in which it's obvious that every sofa, every painting, and every knickknack exists for the sole purpose of aesthetic value or hipster credit. I like a home that looks well loved, a place in which the unique character of its inhabitants is in full evidence—and that means quirks galore, flaws and all. Give me a pad chock full of personality over blandly perfect, hotel-style décor any day, because while physical beauty matters, it's just one small factor in the overall equation for a fabulous home. As you take the steps toward crafting your dream digs, don't get sucked into thinking your home has to look like anything you see in magazines, books, or on television. Real beauty isn't about looks so much as about personality. It's a cliché, sure, though one that's true for homes as well as people.

See, a room that has character appeals to the senses on a level that goes way beyond simple aesthetics: You don't want to look at the space so much as revel in it. Good looks might provide superficial enjoyment but character offers texture. I'm not talking about texture in the literal sense, although it's true that the best rooms have an appealingly touchable quality, featuring fabrics that make you want to run your fingers over them, sofas and chairs and beds that invite you to sink into them, flooring that feels lovely as you shuffle across it in your bare feet. No, furnishings can have texture in a more abstract way, too—through their sense of history and the meaning they possess, those qualities that make you want to pick up the objects, look closer, and find out more. I frequently cite my cheapness as the reason that so many of the objects in my house have been acquired at thrift shops and estate sales. But while that undeniably plays a role, there's another reason I tend to love the old stuff better than the new stuff: I think that objects take on a resonance when they've lived long lives, and I like the time-consuming treasure hunt that goes into finding the *right* old objects for me. I imagine the sort of woman who might have chosen the pristine 1950s sectional sofas that I purchased at an estate sale decades later. I wonder about the unknown artist of the moody abstract landscape painting I picked up at a moving sale. The antique Moroccan rug that sits in my living room is a favorite possession of mine despite the fact that I probably paid way too much for it, and that there's no proof that it's even as old as the salesman in Fez assured. I like the *idea* of the myriad lives that rug has led, regardless of what the truth may be—most of all, I love how the long process by which we came to be suckered into buying that object makes a great story, a hilarious honeymoon memory that my boy and I never tire of relating to folks who comment upon how much they like the rug itself. Yes, my furnishings might match better if I had picked them all up at IKEA; they might not have all those dings in the surfaces or lumps in the cushions. Certainly, it would have taken me a lot less time to accumulate all the pieces, as I could have decked out my whole pad in one big shopping spree. But there's an intrigue that comes from the well-worn secondhand objects that I've snagged here and there that I just don't get from the shiny new goods I see when I wander through a regular retail store. My furniture might not look perfect, but there's character aplenty.

A great sense of character lends an intangible richness to a nest that goes way beyond the more mundane matters of whether the chairs coordinate with the rug. In a nest that has real character, you don't think about the attractiveness of the furnishings but about how much you enjoy spending time there. I had a friend who, before he moved on to greener pastures, lived in a dark, cramped apartment furnished in a mishmash of clashing chairs and sofa sectionals that he'd inherited for free. But his home was a minigallery of his personal history and eclectic passions. Every object in his house had a story behind it—whether it was the oddly pretty, candy-hued plastic virus models perched on the bookshelves (prototypes from his previous life designing natural history exhibits), the exquisitely rendered insect drawings and paintings that practically wallpapered his cinderblock walls, or the Incredible Hulk Halloween candy bucket lurking in the kitchen corner. Compliment any one thing in his home, and you'd most likely trigger a twenty-minute tale of the inevitably fascinating circumstances by which he came to acquire the object, or a detailed explanation of how he decided to make it and why. Getting to know that home was getting to know my friend. His apartment wasn't any interior decorator's notion of a well-decorated home, but it had a weird beauty all its own, and I loved it.

People sometimes seem afraid of weird things, but to me, it's the weird in your abode that make your digs feel most like *your* space. Some of the things I love best in my home are the things that others just don't seem to get. "So what's up with the Astroturf?" a visitor asks, gesturing at the framed blocks of fake lawn, self-expanding insulating foam, fur, caulking, and dripped candle wax that line the wall in our hallway, a tactile art project that the boy and I worked on together. "That's kind of creepy," notes a guest as they point at the blank white Styrofoam heads lining the top of my kitchen, each featuring one of the array of wigs that the boy and I have somehow managed to collect thanks to our penchant for going all-out at costume parties. I know they're odd and that they add to the already significant clutter; I know the house might look neater, and more elegant, if I didn't feel the need to display these strange objects so prominently. But I love these things: I like having them out there in the open where I can enjoy them all the time, and their presence makes perfect sense to the two folks who happen to live among them on a daily basis.

This, in the end, is what really matters when it comes to decorating a home. So maybe "decorating" is a bad way of approaching the process of turning a blank white box of a house into a place in which you can fully, happily live; decorating suggests something superficial, something you do to adorn. Fill your home with things that make you laugh, think, remember, and smile. The difference between a pad that feels like a home and an apartment that's merely a place to house a hodgepodge of belongings has nothing to do with how nice the furnishings are or how cool the wall paint is. It's in whether the décor says something about the folks who live there; it's about a great personality rather than perfect looks.

The thing about personality is that it's something that takes some time to really develop. Creating a pad with character is a process more than a goal. You gradually surround yourself with the stuff that makes you happy and weed out the objects that don't; you learn what colors pep you up and calm you down, and which ones just make you feel claustrophobic. You make mistakes, buying objects that seem way cool at the store and feel totally wrong once you drag them home. You make the bold decision to display that tacky lamp you rescued from the Dumpster, the one that no one else in the world seems to love but you. You put a bit more of yourself into your digs with each curtain you hang, each throw pillow you re-cover, each sofa you rearrange. Little by little, you craft a home that's overflowing with character—specifically, *your* character. Inevitably this process takes time, as you slowly build up a sense of what works best for you, but boy, is the investment worth it.

So quit stressing about whether your pad features the hip color combo du jour, or if your thrift-shopped furnishings are less than perfectly coordinated. Don't fall into a funk if you're looking around at your current apartment and thinking that all the interior design tricks in the world still wouldn't render these particular digs picture-perfect. There's really only one question you need to ask yourself as you take a good look around your pad: Do I dig my life in these here digs? And if the answer's anything less than a "hell yeah," it's time to do something about that. Make the commitment to create digs in which you can sleep, eat, laugh, dream, and live to the very best of your potential—and get ready to take the transformation one little step at a time. Now dig in!

mildew, 247

miniblinds, 119

minigallery, 254

minimalist style, 46

minitask, 34

modern art, *96,* 97

mold, 247

money. *See also* DIY (do it yourself)

    post-college entry level, 64

    as reason for shacking up, 10

    saving, by DIY, 181–82

    for secondhand shopping, 47

    solo living determined by, 9

    to spend on rent, 18–19

    time equaling, 40

mood lighting, 78–79

mop and bucket, 245

multisurface spray cleaner, 248

multitasking furniture, 68, 243–44

National Geographic, 91

natural lighting, 73–74

neat freak, 5

needle-nose pliers, 187

needle-threading, 156–57

neighborhood walk-through, 20

networking, for roomie, 4

noise factor, apartment's, 21

nonnecessities, 45

no-sew tape, 210

office, weeding out junk from, 236–37

oil soap spray, 248

online

apartment hunting, 19

    auctions, 48

    Craigslist.org, 54

    credit card shopping, 55

    DigsMagazine.com, xii

    eBay.com, 54–55

    Freecycle.org, 54

    Google.com, 55

    newspapers, 19

    roomie inquiry, 5

    secondhand shopping, 54–55

online shopping concerns

    about sellers, 55–56

    about transporting of goods, 55

    damaged/misrepresented goods, 56

Oompa Loompa Land, 116

Operation Apartment Furnishing, 25

pack rat, 224

paint

    buying, 145–46

    color theory for choosing, 140–42

    flat and eggshell, 142

    high gloss, 142

    landlords/leases and, 139

    leftover, 147–48

    one-wall-at-a-time thing about, 138

    Paint Chip Thunderdome test for, 140

    picking one's, 138–40

    random colors of, 143

    satin, 142

    semigloss and high gloss, 142

    spray, 149–50, 151–53

    types of finishes, 151

Yee-Fan Sun is the founding editor of DigsMagazine.com, a home and living Web site for the postcollege, preparenthood, quasi-adult generation that has been online since 2000. Since graduating from Harvard University in 1996 and moving away from her home state of Massachusetts, she has lived in Townsville, Australia; Tucson, Arizona; and Edinburgh, Scotland, where she currently shares a house with her husband. Next up is Toronto, where she looks forward to hunting for the perfect pad and setting up new digs—hopefully for the last time in a good long while.